THREADING THE NEEDLE II

J.PRESS

Warren,

a long way from Ellsworth Avenue

Richard

THREADING THE NEEDLE II

*HARRIS TWEED, INDIA MADRAS, AND
THE GOLDEN AGE OF IVY STYLE*

MORE MEMORIES & ANECDOTES
BY RICHARD PRESS

WITH A FOREWORD BY
MARK OPPENHEIMER

J. PRESS
NEW YORK · 2022

Copyright © 2022 by J. Press, Inc.,
and its affiliates and assigns and licensors

All rights reserved

No portion of this book may be reproduced,
stored in a retrieval system, or transmitted in any
form or by any means, mechanical, electronic,
photocopying, recording, or otherwise, without
permission in writing from the publisher.

Printed in the U.S.A.
First edition

Manufacturing by GHP Media
Book design by John Segal

ISBN 979-8-218-06286-6

J. Press Inc./Onward USA LLC
8 West 38th Street, Suite 200
New York, NY 10018

1 2 3 4 5 6 7 8 9 0

CONTENTS

Foreword		IX
Introduction		XV

1.	JACOBI PRESS AND HIS EPISCOPAL CLERGY PALS	17
2.	REVISITING CAMELOT	21
3.	WHEN MAD MEN RULED THE ROOST	24
4.	GROWING UP IN NEW HAVEN	29
5.	BACK ON CAMPUS	31
6.	ANYTHING GOES	33
	DISCOVERIES: JASON JULES	36
7.	A TASTE OF TWEED	38
8.	A QUASI-OFFICIAL YALE MAN	40
9.	IT WAS A VERY GOOD YEAR	43
10.	J. PRESS MERCHANT TAILORS	47
11.	GOLDFINGER ON 44TH ST.	51
12.	THE GOLDEN RULES OF IRVING PRESS	55
	ENDORSEMENT: MATT HRANEK	58
13.	BRIONI, SINATRA & J. PRESS	60
14.	GOLDEN DAYS IN NEW HAVEN	63
15.	MY FAVORITE PROFESSOR	66
16.	TAKING THE MEASURE OF KIM NOVAK	71
17.	THE BELLS TOLL FOR HERMAN	72

CONTENTS

18.	THE FORBIDDEN COLOR OF TRAD	74
19.	THE MAN IN THE 1955 IVY LEAGUE SUIT	76
20.	IVY LIT 101	80
21.	J. PRESS PRIME	83
	RECOLLECTION: DR. JACK CARLSON	86
22.	THE IVY LEAGUE LOOK FOR TODAY	89
23.	WITH POPPY BUSH AND BABE RUTH	91
24.	WHITE DUCKS VS. KHAKI CHINOS	95
25.	STEALING THE HARVARD DRUM	97
26.	YORK STREET SPREZZATURA	100
27.	HEYDAY OF THE IVY LEAGUE SUIT	103
28.	THE BOSS CHATS WITH OL' BLUE EYES	107
29.	TIME MARCHES ON	109
	AN AFFIRMATION: PATRICIA MEARS	112
30.	BELOW NOB HILL	114
31.	THE 2000-YEAR-OLD MAN ON 44TH STREET	117
32.	CYNOSURE OF AMERICAN STYLE	120
33.	POLO SHIRT SPREZZATURA	123
34.	LORD ATTLEE MEETS DICK PRESS	125
35.	FIGHT FIERCELY AT HARVARD	129
	MUSINGS: SCOTT HILL	132
36.	WITH JOHN CHANCELLOR AT THE SUMMIT	135
37.	WE ARE COLLEGE GUYS	137
38.	IN LOVE WITH A SHAGGY DOG	141
39.	THE BEATLES, PINKERTON AND J. PRESS	142

CONTENTS

40.	THE OCBD OSCAR GOES TO J. PRESS	144
41.	BACK TO NEW YORK	147
42.	LUCKY SEVEN IVY ESSENTIALS	149
43.	MR. SATURDAY NIGHT ON YORK STREET	153
	AN APPRECIATION: JOHN BURTON	156
44.	BERMUDAS FOR THE DOG DAYS OF SUMMER	158
45.	BACK AT THE YALE CLUB	160
46.	J. PRESS & ALL THAT JAZZ	163
47.	SALTY VIBES	166
	A MEMORY: BENJAMIN PRESS	168
48.	SUITING UP ELI FROSH	170
49.	INSIDER TRADING AND IRISH OYS	173
50.	IT ALL STARTS WITH A GOOD FOUNDATION	176

Special Thanks   179
Credits   181
About the Author   183

FOREWORD

by Mark Oppenheimer

RICHARD PRESS—actor, producer, bon vivant, husband, father, clothier, raconteur—is heir to perhaps the greatest family name in American men's clothing (sorry, descendants of the brothers Brooks, wherever you are). So one might expect that his essays, produced for the company that bears his grandfather's name, would be about clothing. And they are, up to a point. Aficionados of Bermuda shorts, Oxford-cloth button-down shirts, khakis, blue blazers, madrases, white bucks, and white ducks: Enter here! Step right up! This book is for you. But if you read these bright, witty essays carefully, as one should, you will likely come to the realization that they are only incidentally about clothes. They are really about people and the ties—including bow ties and neckties—that bind them.

It's a truism that you can now buy J. Press clothing online, because of course you can now buy everything online. But these essays are a reminder of how a good men's store, staffed by good people, can provide good times. As with a barbershop or vinyl-record store, one goes for the fellowship as much as for the merchandise. I know that when I stop into my local branch in New Haven, now around the corner from the original York Street branch, where a young Richard Press used to scamper between his dad's and granddad's legs, I come not just for a flap-pocket shirt or Shaggy Dog sweater, but for the happenstance encounter with someone else who is willing to spend a little more to look a lot better.

Have I ever bumped into stars with the candlepower of Duke Ellington or Billy Strayhorn at my J. Press branch? Alas, no. But now I have met them in these columns. They are among the men who have been suited up by J. Press; it will not surprise you that Frank Sinatra was another. Nor even that Kim Novak once stopped by the New York store to mug for the cameras. That stars want good clothing and want to soak up the ambience of its purveyors is the least surprising of news. But clothing stores, as we see, often foster creative commons that have nothing to do with clothes. How else to explain that Ivan Boesky, infamous stock trader, once had a bit part in a play that rehearsed after-hours in J. Press's New York store?

Somehow, it makes perfect sense that Richard Press's grandfather Jacobi, the store's Jewish-immigrant founder, was assisted early in his career by Edward Campion Acheson, the Episcopal bishop of Connecticut and father of a future secretary of state. After all, Ivy League Style was a joint project of Jews and Gentiles, the former at first doing more of the cutting and stitching, the latter modeling the clothing. An alternate title for this book would be, if it weren't already taken, "Protestant Catholic Jew"; its pages are peopled by Jack Kennedy, Bart Giamatti, and no shortage of WASPs, but its vocabulary includes Yiddishisms like pisher, shvitz, and shidduch.

Today, it falls to all of us, of every religious persuasion and none, to row against the current of slovenly indifference. Richard Press is the ultimate democrat. He and his ancestral company offer all people the fabrics and fits, the togs and gear, to spiff up, throw back, or lay back with a bit more style. Good

THREADING THE NEEDLE II

Mark Oppenheimer

men's clothes are not just for the Ivy-educated. Good men's clothes are not even just for men—who among us, no matter our shape or identity, does not smile a bit wider in a well-washed, damned-near-destroyed Oxford-cloth shirt? Good clothes are like good books: when you find them, keep them, fray them, rip them, stain them, love them.

A WORD FROM J. PRESS

IVY STYLE is one of America's most important historical contributions to global fashion, and few brands have had more of a significant impact on Ivy Style than J. Press. At the turn of the 20th century a young tailor named Jacobi Press ventured off on his own to create the eponymous haberdashery J. Press, a tailoring tradition that would help to define the aesthetics of Ivy League Style for over 118 years. As a storied American clothier, J. Press has remained true to the craftsmanship and traditions of its historic past. These traditions continue today at J. Press shops in New York, Washington, D.C., and where it all started, in New Haven.

Generations of men have embraced this vision and passed the J. Press name from father to son. Much in the same way, the company has seen generations of the Press family in the business, most recently Richard Press, who served as company president. It is through Richard that the lore of J. Press is handed down yet again in the following pages of *Threading the Needle Volume II*, our second published collection of his fabled columns. Richard's *Threading the Needle* columns not only preserve the history of the Press family, but also that of New Haven, Ivy Style, and American fashion as a whole.

*To Vida, Jen, Ben, James, Rebecca,
and the grandchildren, great-grandchildren,
and granddogs who have enriched
my life forevermore*

Richard Press

INTRODUCTION

AFTER MANY DECADES in the barn, I am forced to confront a reverse ontological reality: J. Press successfully endures beyond its Press-family origins, but my public fame, however meager, would be even more negligible were it not for the scribblings I devote to the firm Grandpa Press founded 120 years ago.

The columns culled from the encyclopedic collection for inclusion in the current tome—paired with my onstage MC appearances at J. Squeeze events with all their surrounding hoopla—foster both a sense of pride and unmitigated personal joy.

It has been a long journey since my prep-school days as columnist and editor-in-chief of the Loomis (now Loomis Chaffee) Log to my current post, churning out digital spoonfuls of Threading the Needle. Hope you enjoy the flowering remains of the day. There's little more I can add to the thousands of words ahead except to ask fellow readers to consider an advertising jingle popular when I was in the sixth grade:

Sit back, relax, and chew your Dubble Bubble Gum

Jacobi Press

NUMBER 1

JACOBI PRESS AND HIS EPISCOPAL CLERGY PALS

THE SAGA OF J. PRESS began in the Pale of Settlement, the Russian territory in Central Europe decreed by the czar as a residential territory and boundary for the Jews. My grandfather Jacobi, born in 1879, completed his rabbinical studies under the strict supervision of his eldest brother, Rebbe Moishe Gedalia (i.e., Man of God), who chose Jacobi to carry on the Press tradition of producing a rebbe in each generation.

Moishe imposed upon him an unforgiving life of Talmud study that became a torture. Fleeing from the Pale, Jacobi threw out his family rebbe proxy, also affording his brothers and sisters escape from the grinding poverty and ongoing pogroms of the shtetl in Baltromonsk, Latvia.

Jacobi, along with his brothers and sisters, were met in 1896 at the Boston pier by their cousins, who ran a custom-tailor shop in Middletown, Connecticut. Jake immediately bonded with them and quickly mastered the trade. He was a gregarious man who ingratiated himself with the shop's customers, among them Edward Campion Acheson, Episcopal bishop of Connecticut (father of Dean Acheson, who would later become Harry Truman's secretary of state).

Bishop Acheson took a liking to my grandfather, and when Grandpa confided to him that his fiancée didn't want to live in Middletown, Acheson suggested he consider New Haven, a city with a large population of students from Yale University that might offer great opportunity for the ambitious young man. Acheson knew an elderly tailor in New Haven who might be willing to take him on. Bishop Acheson arranged the shidduch (an Orthodox Jewish practice where unmarried men and women are introduced to each other for the purpose of marriage). The shidduch worked, and in 1902 Goldbaum and Press became J. Press, Inc.

A second Episcopal bishop, the Right Reverend Paul Moore Jr., attached himself to my grandfather. In the book My Harvard, My Yale, Moore recalls that after an inebriated night of singing Christmas carols to fellow classmates, he momentarily found himself residing in the New Haven jail. Jacobi Press, his local college tailor, appeared in a three-piece suit with prominent watch chain and derby hat to bail everybody out. Moore recorded that Mr. Press owned a small store on York Street and did more than anyone else to establish the Ivy Look. "We became friends as well as customers of the Press family," he jocularly recalled. "Who else would you telephone from jail at seven o'clock on a Sunday morning? Not your father, not your college master, God knows. So you called J. Press."

Another reverend, Yale chaplain Sidney Lovett, became Grandpa's confidant. Sid Lovett was a spare man, his tweed suits loosely strewn on his granite features. "Uncle Sid," he told me to call him. He was also a fishing partner along with my grandfather's immigrant Jewish cronies on Captain Al's boat in Branford.

I was thirteen years old when Grandpa Press died. Uncle Sid gently placed a New Haven pond lily on the coffin. The funeral was performed in Mishkan Israel's Moorish-styled temple, which was originally the Third Congregational Church of New Haven, Grandpa's final joust against Jewish Orthodoxy.

"Paul," Uncle Sid told my father, "when I said goodbye to him, I simply said, so long Joe Press." Sid always called my grandfather "Joe Press."

Faith of our Fathers! Holy faith!
We will be true to thee till death.

"He is the best-dressed president since Grover Cleveland."

NUMBER 2

REVISITING CAMELOT

THE TRAGIC CHORD of President John F. Kennedy's epic saga that ended nearly sixty years ago remains an everlasting fugue on the dark side of the American soul. The week following the assassination, Jackie Kennedy fed *Life* magazine journalist Teddy White her version of their time in the White House, equating it with the Arthurian legend of Camelot, as if to insist that light shone on the Kennedy administration. Historians may differ regarding the validity of her version. Mrs. Kennedy would have hesitated to recognize the private battle that occurred in the "War of the Tailors," jousting one another in the battle to dress the king.

While Kennedy was at Harvard, his father was named U.S. ambassador to England and steered him to his longtime Savile Row tailor, H. Harris. Harris maintained a New York branch on 57th Street run by third-generation family member Sam Harris. Seven months after Kennedy's inauguration, "Tailor" Sam Harris, as he was condescendingly described in *Life* magazine, disclosed intimate wardrobe details of his most prominent customer. Harris concluded his comments with a benediction from hell: "He is the best dressed president since Grover Cleveland. We made his suits too." There were no more "happily ever afterings" in Camelot for Sam Harris.

This was all undisclosed to the public, but Frank Brothers Fenn-Feinstein leaked to a Connecticut newspaper that the president had got rid of his tailor because of the *Life* article. Fenn-Feinstein, whose client roster included Kennedy brother-in-law Sargent Shriver and Governor Abraham Ribicoff, speculated that J.F.K. might come on board.

The gossip prompted Irving Press and my father, Paul, to enter the fray to outfit the president. They lobbied the many J. Press customers and friends in the Kennedy circle. The top tier included journalist Charlie Bartlett, who introduced Jack to Jackie; Hyannis Port regular Chuck Spalding; Harvard professor and White House staffer Arthur Schlesinger Jr.; F.A.A. head Najeeb Halaby; Foreign Affairs Adviser Bill Bundy; J.F.K. personal photographer Mark Shaw; and chairman of J.F.K.'s Council of Economic Advisors Walter Heller.

Chipp won by default. Their stalwarts included brother Bobby; Lem Billings; Defense Secretary Robert McNamara; brothers-in-law actor Peter Lawford and Steve Smith; and Papa Kennedy's financial guru, Sid Winston. His son Paul and master fitter Bob DiFalco began to include the White House on their finished-garment schedule.

Kennedy enjoyed a brief encounter with J. Press during his short stay at Princeton, spending much of his time plagued with illness before dropping out mid-term and entering Harvard the following fall. Kirk LeMoyne Billings was his best friend and roommate since their prep-school years at Choate. "Lem" Billings fulfilled the paradigm of elite WASP man-about-town. Bearing proper Pittsburgh-society credentials, he sported spiffy tweeds and bold flannels in contrast to his pal J.F.K., who slinked around Nassau Hall clad in studied indifference. The duo was hooked on becoming companion and customer of the

THREADING THE NEEDLE II

JFK at Harvard

astute Lou Prager, a bon vivant man-about-town, campus celebrity, and manager of the J. Press Princeton branch on 5 Palmer Square. More of a club than a store, Prager catered to the sartorial and social whims of many Princetonians, affirming 5 Palmer as the off-campus faux eating, drinking, and shopping club of the campus cognoscenti.

NUMBER 3

WHEN MAD MEN RULED THE ROOST

THE PARTY'S OVER. Madison Avenue sidewalks, bare of shoppers, remain a ghostlike remnant of the celebrated *"Mad Men"* era, when teeming shoppers and classy shops were stuffed like salamis north of 44th Street. Americana period-drama television series *Mad Men* ran a fabled take of the era on AMC from 2007 to 2015.

"Mad Men" was a slang term that 1950s admen working on Madison Avenue used to refer to themselves, "Mad" being short for "Madison Avenue."

The series protagonist, Don Draper (Jon Hamm), was a womanizing, hard-drinking, chain-smoking emblem of the times. He and his bros arrogantly marched up and down Madison Avenue, flaunting their grey suits tailored in a variety of shoulder styles, from three-button natural to two-button square. Adjacent shops in the quadrant of 44th Street to 57th served them well.

A classic romantic-comedy-drama, Billy Wilder's 1960 film *The Apartment*, further epitomized the epoch starring occasional J. Press customer (since his Harvard days) Jack Lemmon. Drawing a bead climbing the executive ladder, 1960s corporate amorality ruled the roost with scenarios chronicling pre–Harvey Weinstein #MeToo aggressions.

Caravans of Mad Men admen boozers hoisted three-hour

martini lunches at the Gamecock on 44th Street between Fifth and Madison. The 1961 J. Squeeze New York store above the fray was squeezed in a toothpaste-tube location at the northwest corner of Madison and 44th Street.

The offbeat location around the corner from the legendary preppy gathering place, Clock at the Biltmore, at school vacation and cash-sale times provided a line of wannabes from the Squeeze elevator all the way out the door to the sidewalk. The narrow space was coming apart at the seams when Harry Macklowe, a pushy lease dealer prior to becoming an incendiary real-estate mogul, strutted off the elevator. "I'm gonna make a deal," he told Irving Press, "to move you downstairs to the other side of Madison into the space currently occupied by the Atlantic Coast Railroad."

Harry got us out of our lease at the right time in booming 1962 Camelot. The first-floor selling space was 3,200 square feet with Ivy Style window displays on the street utilizing their full six-foot depth. Irving copied the window format of his New Haven–York Street headquarters. During frequent travels to England, he drew inspiration from window displays he studied in London's Burlington Arcade.

The new quarters were also next door to the Gamecock. Irving Press savored his chops upstaging competitor Chipp, owned by former J. Press employees occupying second-floor quarters upstairs from the booming saloon below, and no sidewalk window displays to highlight their "go to hell," otherwise famous pants.

Brooks Brothers held forth its leadership role in its multi-storied 1912 landmark building at 346 Madison with Paul Stuart a block away harboring a mid-block location on 45th Street. Paul Stuart's clothing was manufactured by Grieco Brothers–

THREADING THE NEEDLE II

Southwick, utilizing the same make as its mid-priced neighbor, sixth-floor Brooks Brothers labeling Stuart the "poor man's Brooks Brothers." New Haven tailor Arthur M. Rosenberg burrowed across the street next door to romantic Abercrombie & Fitch, highlighting their unlikely combination of hunting and safari gear together with soft-shoulder, three-button Ivy. Moving uptown, F.R. Tripler at 46th and Madison pushed a quantity of goods manufactured in upstate Rochester by its former owner Hickey Freeman, featuring square-shouldered, corporate, pseudo-formal wardrobes. Rex Harrison's My Fair Lady New Haven custom tailor Rosenthal-Maretz faced Hamburger Heaven (popular with the office staff) on 54th Street. J. Press New Haven neighbor Fenn-Feinstein was situated west of Madison on 57th Street. This retail ambiance occurred at the time salesman Ralph Lauren was pushing cravats behind the tie counters at Brook Brothers and with Fred Pressman was dynamically marketing off-price quality goods in his Barneys family emporium on 17th Street.

I may have left out or forgot some key players, but octogenarian memory goes only so far. Don Draper and his guys poured cash into all the nearby clothing parlors, enabling *Mad Men* sartorial armor. Draper offers the final take:

> *Nostalgia—it's delicate but potent ... Teddy told me in Greek nostalgia literally means "the pain from an old wound." It's a twinge in your heart far more powerful than memory alone.*

NUMBER 4

GROWING UP IN NEW HAVEN

THE TITLE OF PHILIP ROTH'S 1959 novella, *Goodbye, Columbus*, refers to a disc recording awarded to graduating Ohio State seniors that evoked songs, cheers, and the nostalgia of their bright college years—the weakest among them played on iPhones into their grave. It almost happened to me, having grown up next to the Yale campus and immersed in Eli popular culture, together with the campus sartorial legacy of our family business, J. Press—the mixed metaphor of my life. I never chanted "Boola Boola," instead escaping childhood fantasies at Dartmouth. Growing up in a college town—be it New Haven, Hanover, Ithaca, Charlottesville, or whatever—stays with you forever.

In 1940s New Haven, classmates at my public elementary school came from surrounding Irish, Italian, and Jewish neighborhoods. I never enjoyed a WASP peer until my parents sent me to New Haven's historic Hopkins day school for seventh- and-eighth-grade preparation for boarding school at Loomis Chaffee. I left home for Dartmouth to escape my Dodge City years growing up surrounded by all those Skull and Boners.

Me and my pals were regulars at all the Bulldog athletic events. Heroes included Levi Jackson, former star at Hillhouse High School prior to entering Yale. His father was a dining-room steward at the college. Jackson became the first black football captain in the Ivy League. My father once furnished a birthday treat by bringing Jackson with us to the fabled Louis' Lunch, alleged U.S. home of the hamburger. I was so excited that I threw up in the men's room.

I also worshipped the balletic hook shots of all-American basketball star Tony Lavelli, a scholarship kid from Somerville, Massachusetts, who made pocket change playing the accordion at the Loew's Poli movie palace before the preview, cartoon, and newsreel. And not to forget George H. W. "Poppy" Bush, the Yale baseball captain.

Not only sports. My best friend and I howled alongside arrogant Yalies at a Shubert Theatre try-out, hysterically booing alcoholic Yale movie star Sonny Tufts when he drunkenly forgot his lines and mangled dance routines in *Ankles Aweigh*, the dreadful burlesque musical. Poor Sonny was immediately replaced, but the show still flopped on Broadway.

New Haven stays in my blood more than half a century removed from the old hometown. Especially the memory of Grandpa Press's funeral service at Temple Mishkan Israel. His longtime pal and fishing companion, Yale chaplain and pastor of the Church of Christ at Yale Sid Lovett, left our family pew, gently placing a New Haven pond lily upon my grandfather's open coffin.

Goodbye, Columbus.

NUMBER 5

BACK ON CAMPUS

NEARLY NINE YEARS SINCE they had to vacate their longtime York Street home due to damage from a winter storm, J. Press is returning to the Yale campus's Broadway area. The store will take over the Elm Street space formerly occupied by Tyco printers.

My recollection of visits to the building brings back heart-rending memories of growing up as a kid in New Haven. The 1940s and 1950s WELI *Jukebox Saturday Night* weekend radio broadcasts featured a local celebrity disc jockey pushing hit 78-r.p.m. records available in listening booths at the David Dean Smith Record and Phonograph Shop, which occupied the site of the soon-to-be J. Press New Haven headquarters.

Pre-adolescents, high-school kids, and even a few Yalies lined up down the block to gain entrance, spinning singles of Frankie Laine belting "Mule Train" or Miss Peggy Lee warbling "Baubles, Bangles and Beads."

The Yankee Doodle Coffee and Sandwich Shop occupied the York Street side of the building beginning in 1950, before closing its doors in 2008. The narrow restaurant with only 12 stools—arranged along a counter that ran the length of the shop—was a favorite among students, faculty, and assorted Eli hangers-on. In a previous account, I recalled my dad, Paul Press,

Architect's rendering of the new J. Press store

president of his temple, escorting the Reverend Dr. Martin Luther King Jr. to the Doodle to quaff cheeseburgers and chocolate milkshakes prior to a one-on-one tour of J. Press, before finally heading to the New Haven railroad station after M.L.K.'s talk at Mishkan Israel.

Can't wait for the campus rejuvenation, with the building's backyard overlooking the still J. Press–owned 262 York Street space, adjacent to the architectural Georgian ambiance of Yale's Davenport College.

NUMBER 6

ANYTHING GOES

DURING A 1912 FOOTBALL GAME at Yale Field, just across the street from where the Yale Bowl was being constructed and would open the following year, Cole Porter joined the band for the halftime march down the gridiron to introduce his new Yale fight song, "Bulldog." "Bulldog, bulldog, bow-wow-wow, Eli Yale." By the time the game was over, Porter and his Delta Kappa Epsilon band of brothers were well lubricated and had spotted a Chapel Street trolley passing the stadium. Porter gave the cry: "Hijack!"

A "Keystone Cop" chase ensued to York Street, where Porter leaped out of the trolley and ran to J. Press next to the D.K.E. house. Inside, my grandfather hid him in the store cellar until the coast was clear.

Jacobi Press and Cole Porter are both long gone, but a commemorative line has stayed in *Anything Goes*, frequently revived since it first opened, in 1932. In one scene, standing on a set designed to be the deck of an ocean liner, the romantic lead throws a stuffed animal to his drunk boss, who is heading for the Henley Regatta to cheer for Yale. "Here, Boss," he says, "I got you the bulldog at J. Press."

The following year, Cole Porter, along with fellow Yalie Dean Acheson, roomed together at Harvard Law School. Porter eventually abandoned law to return to music, but years later, while

Porter even gave the cry: "Hijack!"

serving as secretary of state in the Truman administration, Acheson, renowned for his elegant wardrobe, was featured in a 1949 Life magazine half-page portrait, attributing his suit to J. Press.

The title song from Cole Porter's 1932 Broadway hit still rings a bell:

> *And those blues you've got*
> *From those news you've got*
> *And those pains you've got*
> *(If any brains you've got)*
> *From those little radios*
> *Anything goes.*

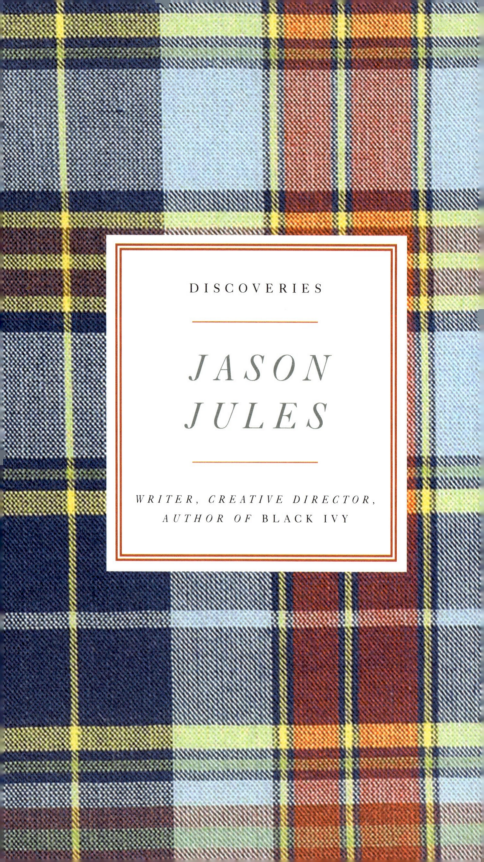

DISCOVERIES

JASON JULES

WRITER, CREATIVE DIRECTOR, AUTHOR OF BLACK IVY

THE J. PRESS STORE *is one of those places you grow up hearing about, a kind of mythical destination you include on your bucket list never really believing you'll ever get to visit it or even own one of their pieces. At least that's how it is if you're a working-class teen from East London and the furthest you've ever traveled out of the country is a disastrous school trip to France.*

Maybe that's why I still look back at my first J. Press purchase, or should I say "find" with such fondness.

It was a seersucker jacket, half-lined with three buttons and lightly padded shoulders. I stumbled across it in a store on the Kings Road that sold American vintage and antique stuff. It was in pristine condition or, as the salesman said, "in perfect nick."

Back then I was organizing nightclubs featuring rare grove and funk music with DJs like Norman Jay and Jazzie B from Soul 2 Soul in London's West End.

Even though most of the kids who attended these clubs wore a mix of flared jeans, Afro wigs, disco-style platform shoe,s and balloon-sleeve shirts, somehow I was the one who seemed to be dressed the most weird and least comprehensible, in my Madras shorts, penny loafers, polo shirts … and this amazing seersucker jacket.

NUMBER 7

A TASTE OF TWEED

GROWING UP IN POST–WORLD WAR II NEW HAVEN, being a "tweedy guy" meant membership in a coterie of self-designated social elites. As the trust-fund student population dwindled, enlisting a wider campus-population base during the 1960s, the Ivy League became less engaged with the snobby wardrobe credentials of past generations. Even storied horn-rimmed, briar-pipe-smoking professors in three-piece tweed suits took a hit.

Suits are currently the domain of male TV anchors, bank tellers, and morticians. Sport jackets provide the answer for situations when suits are not required yet a modicum of dignity needs to be maintained. The dress code of the august University Club of New York states, "Gentlemen members and guests are required to wear a jacket and dress shirt."

Classic navy blazers remain the go-to jacket, but let me suggest their repetitive mode is quite simply becoming a bore. J. Press fills the void with an abundant inventory of Moorish tweeds. Two resources arrived on our racks years ago when Irving Press's perambulations in the British Isles brought home the bacon.

Magee Irish Donegal homespun tweeds in exclusive J. Press patterns and designs, the peerless mixture of Irish wool and

THREADING THE NEEDLE II

A whiff of the fabric still emits a lingering peaty remnant of its crottle-lichen dyes.

imported mohair and cashmere, offer a sophisticated blend of coloring and lush comfort together with a matchless bloom and luxurious touch.

Harris Tweeds earmarked especially for J. Press impart the hardy robust character and inimitable earthy colorings woven by hand in the Outer Hebrides Isles, off the western coast of Scotland. Derived from special mid-weight yarns dyed with indigenous island vegetation, they present a look and feel unlike any other. Also, the smell. A whiff of the fabric still emits a lingering peaty remnant of its crottle-lichen dyes.

You don't need to be tapped for Skull and Bones to be tweedy. C'mon down to J. Squeeze to field the scrum.

NUMBER 8

A QUASI-OFFICIAL YALE MAN

TWO RECENT POSTS sent my way from J. Press fandom that I haven't seen in ages. First and foremost, the enclosed picture of my dad, Paul Press, at his York Street headquarters, circa 1982. Next in line, Mollie Wilson's interview that appeared in *The Yale Journal for Humanities in Medicine* two years before his death in 2006, three days short of his 95th birthday.

The article recounted several anecdotes endlessly repeated in my presence. It seems that in the 1950s, when the then recently formed (now deceased) Woodbridge Country Club was looking to establish a dress code, club president Morris Bailey (owner-manager of New Haven's Shubert Theatre) naturally turned to resident haberdashery expert Paul Press for guidance. My dad and Bailey disagreed when it came to the acceptability of Bermuda golf shorts. Dad was in favor of allowing them while the more aggressive Bailey declared short pants permissible only for swimwear. The issue was still undecided when Senator Prescott Bush, father and grandfather of Presidents George H. W. and George W., respectively, showed up at the club for lunch and a golf date with my beloved uncle, Judge Harold E. Alprovis, then chairman of Bush's senatorial campaign. My father painted an indelible picture of the scene, warming up to the punch line when he asked my uncle, "Where's the senator?"

Paul Press, "quasi-official part of Yale."

"He's downstairs in the locker room getting dressed," my uncle replied. Shortly thereafter, stealing the show, six-foot-four Senator Prescott Bush, elegantly clad in walk shorts, appeared with no further comment necessary, settling the debate. "They wore shorts after that" became the Senator Bush and Paul Press dictum.

J. PRESS

My dad had a good word for just about anybody he met in the portals of 262 York Street. He broadcast the friendship of all recent Yale presidents, recounting to anyone within earshot, "Kingman Brewster was a hell of a fine fellow, and so was Whitney Griswold," and describing Benno Schmidt's father as a young entrepreneur who made lucrative deals for J. H. Whitney in postwar orange-juice sales. Dad reserved special praise, however, for A. Bartlett Giamatti, whom he counted as a close friend. Valentine Giamatti, Bart's father, was one of Dad's Hillhouse High classmates, and both were seated together at Bart's inauguration. When Yale purchased the Jewish Community Center on Chapel Street, in 1978, Dad chastised the younger Giamatti, "You have deprived me of my fitness center!"

"Don't worry about it, Paul," the future commissioner of baseball said. "You'll belong to the Yale gym."

"I'm not a graduate of Yale," Dad reminded his friend. Giamatti waved away the protest, and before long Dad received a letter that, later, he would regularly recite from memory: "You're a quasi-official part of Yale, and we're delighted to give you a membership in the Yale gym."

He regularly worked out on the Nautilus machines and swam multitude laps in the pool at the Payne Whitney, blocks from 262 York Street. Paul Press never finished his story without pridefully displaying the membership card that identifies his status as "special."

"See? I'm special," he would say, grinning before anyone he cornered with the story.

For God, for Country, and for Eli Yale.

NUMBER 9

IT WAS A VERY GOOD YEAR

FRANK SINATRA SPORTED J. Press Ivy in 1969. It was a very good year. Sinatra's gone, but J. Press Ivy is still here and thriving. Sinatra found himself drawn to the staples in the J. Press product line—especially blue blazers. By my estimate he must have ordered about a dozen of them from us—four or five with his first order of suits, and one or two each time he would come to the store to order new clothes. Explaining that the blazers also needed to be appropriate for the climate of Southern California, he was especially partial to the easy drape of our doeskin flannel (a mid-weight 11–12 oz.) as well as to the pure cashmere model that iconic fitter Felix Samelson reworked with hand-sewn edges, and several more durable worsted jackets "for the plane."

It helped to keep things running smoothly on the business end with J. Press that Sinatra's taste in suits and jackets was refined, his knowledge of fabrics extensive, and his marching orders to us succinct. I took notes, both in real time for Felix and, as it turns out, for posterity: "Three-on-two-button stance for all the jackets. If I unbutton the coat, I want the collar roll to the lapel from the middle button. I never button the top one. I always show 3/8-inch of the shirt sleeve. Cuff the pants clean to the tip of my shoes and take out all suspender buttons. I'm a belt guy."

"Orange is the happiest color."

THREADING THE NEEDLE II

Felix always maintained that, compared with the intricate and exacting demands of our hairsplitting, overly officious bespoke customers, Sinatra's instructions were straight ahead, easy to follow, and consistent with someone who had undergone extensive fittings for suits and accessories over the course of a thirty-year professional career. It helped the master tailor to relax considerably when, as a new customer, Sinatra barked, "Stash the chalk—it's perfect," after returning and deciding he needed to try on only the first of the half-dozen suits Felix had altered for him. As he buttoned the herringbone tweed suit, he said to me, "Hey, Richie, do I look like I went to Yale?"

During a solo visit to J. Press, a short time after his initial suit-fitting, Sinatra shouted over to me, "Now what else do you have in this joint to show me?"

I led Sinatra on a tour of the store, and he eagerly picked out sport coats, ties, Oxford button-down shirts, Shaggy Dog sweaters, Argyle socks, and anything we had in orange—pocket squares, sweaters, and sweater vests. One of his pals explained that Sinatra had a special love of all things orange, a color he considered to be "upbeat." His California home was said to be decorated in an array of orange hues.

"Put together what goes with 'em. Same stuff you sell to your Yale big shots."

Even with Sinatra it always comes back to J. Press and Yale. Over a few Jack Daniel's, he once mocked me: "Hey, Richie, how the hell did you find any broads in the woods up at Dartmouth?"

"Frank," I told him, "I did it my way."

He threw me the 25-ounce J. Press Saxony herringbone tweed double-breasted guardsman overcoat. Frank had retrieved it for me while making a final sweep of Frank Jr.'s dressing room after we'd all departed. "Hey, Richie," said Sinatra, "get me one of these Winston Churchills."

Toots Shor's was a sports saloon and restaurant that had the unmistakable feel of a men's club. Regulars included Walter Cronkite, Chief Justice Earl Warren, Joe DiMaggio, Jackie Gleason, Mike Wallace, Yogi Berra, Edward R. Murrow, gangster Frank Costello, and Jimmy Hoffa. The joint was presided over by perhaps one of the most illustrious and quintessential New York hosts who ever lived, Bernard "Toots" Shor.

For Toots Shor, whose cronies he famously called "crumb bums," Sinatra's presence seemed to transform the night into a real happening. He punctuated a bear hug for his old pal with a sloppy, wet kiss, and our third stop of the evening was off to the races. Unfortunately for future Sinatra historians, my memory of the early morning at the storied saloon is hazy at best and becomes more of a drunken blur as the evening wore on. As Toots Shor himself often said, "A bum who ain't drunk by midnight ain't trying," and this bum had been drunk well before midnight. I vaguely remember the harsh bright lights coming on at closing time and hearing subsequent reports of Sinatra's security guy practically carrying me out of the establishment and pouring me into a taxicab.

No, no they can't take that away from me.

NUMBER 10

J. PRESS MERCHANT TAILORS

TAILORING WAS ALMOST AN ACCIDENT for my grandfather Jacobi Press, but not quite. He arrived in Boston Harbor with his three sisters in 1896. They were met at the pier by his brothers, Max and Harry, who had settled earlier, establishing a small custom-tailor shop in Middletown, Connecticut. "Jake," as he was called by the family, learned English at age 16 (without an accent) by assisting the shop's customers while, at the same time, working with an old German tailor they employed. It was from him that Jacobi learned the art of cutting and design, in between delivering packages to help pay his way.

Jacobi's big break came in 1902. Since the Civil War, merchant tailor Herman Goldbaum had owned and operated a shop at 150 Elm Street, just off the Yale campus in downtown New Haven. The turn of the twentieth century found Mr. Goldbaum embroiled in debt and looking for a way out of his financial predicament. A future partnership agreement was negotiated, pursuant to Press's bringing in enough new business to settle Goldbaum's financial abyss.

How to bring in the customers? My grandfather mustered up enough courage to knock on a dormitory door one afternoon. At first the boys laughed at him, but before he was through he had most of them as customers. According to family lore, Grandpa once snatched a suit jacket off a dissatisfied student customer during a fitting, telling him, "If you don't like the way it fits, then I own it. It's mine, and you don't have to pay for it."

The training he received at his brothers' Middletown emporium provided Jacobi Press enough tailoring experience to process all the new orders he brought in. He was a dapper man, carefully decked out in three-piece English woolens, an astute wardrobe in the manner of debonair Professor William Lyon Phelps and other well-dressed notables on the Yale campus. He adopted the gift of gab and quick sense of humor he'd observed among the high club echelons en route to their elite social gatherings. The original Goldbaum obligations were fully paid by 1908. Goldbaum & Press was dissolved in an amiable manner. No lawyers were needed to assist the transaction. The partners simply flipped a coin for each piece of goods, shook hands, and divided the remaining assets.

"Men like Lewis Douglas, our present Ambassador to England, still have their clothes tailored by Press," a 1949 *Custom Tailor Magazine* reported. "Former Ambassador to the Soviet Union, now Marshall Plan Envoy W. Averell Harriman, heir to the Union Pacific fortune, fondly recalls when Jacobi Press lent him 25 cents for breakfast after an expensive weekend. In fact, the Press firm's ledgers read like an unabridged version of Who's Who in American life that also includes Secretary-of-State Dean Acheson."

My induction into the family business occurred when I joined the firm shortly after graduating college. I was brought onto the scene during an emergency. The J. Press southern road traveler was taken ill, and I was called off the bench to fill in for him. The most traumatic obligation thrust upon me was fitting a basted try-on in Charlottesville, Virginia, for Colgate W.

Bespoke expertise continues today at our stores.

Darden, Jr., dean of the University of Virginia Medical School. A basted try-on prepares the needlework of a garment for sewing. I didn't know how to read a tape measure, let alone pin a suit. Even worse, the fitting was for white tie and tails that the customer was planning to wear for a gala event at Monticello.

Ralph Chieffo was the chief fitter and designer at the New Haven York Street headquarters. Before his career at J. Press, he operated a custom-tailoring school in New Haven and wrote the textbook *How to Tailor a Custom Suit*. He quickly gave me an emergency tutorial. Dr. Darden later told Ray Jacobs, the southern traveler, to send his regards to the young Mr. Press for his fluent fitting debut.

Bespoke expertise continues today at our stores, the all-star list of our roster remains confidential, unlike the dubious celebrity wardrobes bragged about in digital media. In a public age we respect the privacy of our patrons. The invaluable experience of 120 years of successful merchant tailoring underlies our unique facility for tailoring superlative clothes to individual order. Our Made to Measure tailored-clothing program combines expert tailoring with personal specifications and a wide selection of fabrics from the finest mills. J. Press custom shirts offer the same unique resources as our clothing department. My uncle Irving Press regularly availed himself of the opportunity to choose button-down shirts with sleeves able to accommodate his treasured gold-frame IEP cuff links. In a similar manner, many prefer point, club, or English tab collars, or various combinations of contrast collar and cuffs not usually available in ready-to-wear shirts.

That is the true legacy of Jacobi Press. Our dedicated staff adheres fervently to the golden rule of customer satisfaction that has been our touchstone since 1902.

NUMBER 11

GOLDFINGER ON 44TH STREET

THE CURRENT TREND among crooks and Russian oligarchs laundering 800 grand a year on their threads touched memory lane regarding my all-time favorite J. Press big shot.

Charles Engelhard Jr. established the gold standard of elegance at J. Press.

Engelhard's wardrobe alliance began in the mid-1930s at St. Paul's School, where he patronized the regular J. Press travel exhibits and continued at the shop on Nassau Street while he attended Princeton, graduating in 1939. Upon the death of his father, in 1950, he inherited the family business and substantially expanded operations in South Africa, South America, and Europe, becoming one of the world's leading refiners of precious metals.

In a 1969 feature article, *Sports Illustrated* tabbed him "the Platinum King," mogul of a vast economic empire, who found joy in Coca-Cola, Hershey's Kisses, and a multimillion-dollar stable competing on three continents. The quote depicting his sprezzatura: "That morning in the Aiken, South Carolina, stable Engelhard was sockless, his feet dipped in fleece-lined hide boots. He wore two sweaters, a bulky scarlet and a blue which rolled and bunched over mustard slacks—disordered clothing that would hardly fit the image of an international tycoon."

Engelhard's forays at J. Press occurred every January.

Whenever Mr. Engelhard got off the elevator at 44th Street, Walter Napoleon, star salesman and manager of the New York store, made certain there were plenty of iced Coca-Colas and a bowl of Hershey's Kisses next to the swatches. One day, however, he had an experience much less sweet.

Mr. Engelhard (as he was always called) was in the midst of his annual winter visit when a worker crashed through a fake ceiling with the air-conditioning unit he was installing, both landing between Engelhard and Walter Napoleon. Bolts of woolens together with piles of swatch books were strewn around the wreckage between the two, yet miraculously nobody was hurt. Mr. Napoleon kept his pad and pencil out, and, not missing a beat, Charlie continued to mark and select swatches.

The 1964 James Bond movie, *Goldfinger*, adapted from Ian Fleming's spy thriller of the same name, brought Engelhard unwanted celebrity. A man for all seasons, Fleming was an author, a journalist, and a former British investigator in World War II. He was also a longtime Engelhard pal familiar with Engelhard's intricate mineral and financial machinations, and modeled arch-fiend Auric Goldfinger on Mr. Engelhard.

Engelhard's forays at J. Press occurred every January, with final try-ons slated for the middle of March. During that time, legions of tailors in the shops of New York and New Haven devoted their energies to finishing the extensive order, with extra cloth available to meet the demanding requirements of his President William Howard Taft–esque body proportions.

Engelhard's annual order—multiple quantities of overcoats, topcoats, suits, sport coats, blazers, and trousers, with all the trappings of furnishings and haberdashery—were equally shipped to Cragwood Stables, his estate in Far Hills, New Jersey; the Waldorf Towers in New York; apartments in London and Rome; the Dolder Grand Hotel in Zurich; the mansion in Johannesburg; the lodge in the lion country of the Eastern Transvaal; salmon camp in Gaspé, Quebec; and his beach house in Boca Grande, Florida. Additional sport and warm-weather gear went to the horse farms, fishing camps, hunting lodges, and whatever other venue required special treatment.

Every detail was carefully supervised by his wife, Jane, a brilliant "Best-Dressed" woman whom the New York society pages affectionately called "Our Mother Superior." Mrs. Engelhard once brought a men's size-52 mink coat, directing me to attach it to the lining of a Burberry trench coat, a birthday gift for her husband. She ordered a full range of custom suits every Christmas for Derek, her husband's valet.

In 1967, I received an emergency call from her, informing me that she and her husband were leaving on Air Force One with President Lyndon Johnson to attend the state funeral for Australian prime minister Harold Holt, who had tragically drowned that morning. Her husband had gained weight since he last wore funeral garments, and Derek would deliver them to the store pronto. She was confident that Felix Samelson, our master fitter, would understand what alterations would be required, sight unseen. Derek would leave the following morning on the Engelhard private plane to deliver the garments on time for the event.

When her husband died, on March 17, 1971, at their house in Boca Grande, Mrs. Engelhard called to tell me she would be honored if Felix, my Uncle Irving, and I would be her guests at the funeral. Irving was traveling in Europe, but we were seated in the pews of St. Mary's Abbey Church in Morris Township, New Jersey, alongside former president Johnson, former vice president Hubert Humphrey, Senator Ted Kennedy, and Senate Majority Leader Mike Mansfield.

Goldfinger was the man with the "Midas touch," but Charlie Engelhard brought home the bacon at J. Press with a touch of Ivy class.

NUMBER 12

THE GOLDEN RULES OF IRVING PRESS

BACK IN 1959, when I entered the family business at the J. Press New York store, Uncle Irving Press took me to lunch at the Yale Club, a custom he followed when hiring each salesperson at his 44th Street store. Together with the Grill Room lunch he fed me were his golden rules:

1. Study the current J. Press brochure and learn it by heart.

2. Respect your customer. He (or she) didn't come to J. Press to socialize with you. No first names. When you finish the transaction (even without a purchase), offer your card, letting the customer know you would be pleased to serve him or her again.

3. Ask if they have received the J. Press brochure and, if not, offer to put them on the mailing list.

4. Ask how they got to J. Press, whether we'd been suggested by any friends, classmates, business associates, or relatives who favored the store.

5. Don't be afraid to suggest additional merchandise selections. Know your stock well enough to provide the history and

Richard and Irving Press at the Yale Club.

derivation of each garment, as well as the wearing qualities and style details.

6. Review each day's customer transactions. Memorize their names, whatever personal history was disclosed. Note their clothing preferences. Learn what brought them into the store—classmates, friends, business associates, magazine or newspaper ads.

Irving positioned me at the front door to greet prospective customers. My routine: "Hi, I'm Richard Press. Welcome to J. Press. How may we help you?" If they care just to look around, say, "Suits are in the back," point to the sport coats and trousers,

The golden rules of Irving Press still hold fast.

and offer this sage advice: "Don't be afraid to mess up the ties. They're here to be explored, felt, and touched." If the prospective patron needs further attention, steer him or her to the next salesperson "on call."

The golden rules of Irving Press still hold fast at the institution bearing his father's name. Times may have changed, but J. Press is nearly alone promoting American style in our historic specialty stores that continue to honor tireless customer service, careful attention to all details of production and craft, realistic pricing, and unstinting recognition of the superior taste of a demanding but unfailingly loyal clientele.

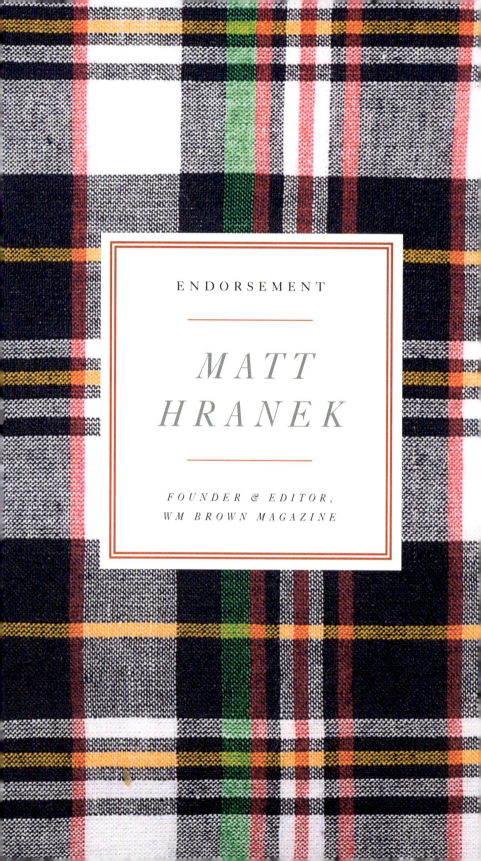

ENDORSEMENT

MATT HRANEK

*FOUNDER & EDITOR,
WM BROWN MAGAZINE*

J. PRESS, TO ME, *is the mecca for madras. I have been reasonably obsessed with madras (Patch Madras to be exact) since my high-school days . (And that has been a while now, trust me.) I grew up in the preppy Northeast, a place where the Original Preppy Handbook was your bible. My style has not changed much from those days except for the quality of fits and materials, and J. Press has been my steady supplier of madras (and patch madras) since I discovered the shop in Mid-town when I moved to NYC years ago. I own shirts, shorts, and jackets from J. Press, but my absolute coveted madras item from the shop are my patch madras trousers—tapered narrow to the ankle and hemmed high with no break, they are the perfect summer pant that are brilliantly diverse, comfortable, and wearable. They look great barefoot at a beach BBQ with a polo as well as with a navy DB blazer and a pair of well-worn Gucci loafers or Belgians. To me, these pants will always mean summer, and I wear them to death until they are stored away for another summer season—promptly on Labor Day.*

NUMBER 13

BRIONI, SINATRA & J. PRESS

G. BRUCE BOYER, pal and acknowledged menswear authority, recently queried me about J. Press and Brioni. He disclosed a recent conversation with Joe Barrato, wondering if I knew him.

Mr. Barrato recently published an entertaining book, *Beyond Category*, which details his personal career path, including his two decades as C.E.O. and president of Brioni U.S.A.

Barrato, whom I met years ago, told Bruce that Brioni had made some suits for J. Press and that Frank Sinatra bought one. Proof of the pudding, he produced a store receipt from our Mad Men quarters oat 16 East 44th Street.

The February 24, 1969, sale reveals Sinatra to have been a canny buyer, purchasing the suit at a reduced price. The sales slip was transcribed by star salesperson Ken Trommers. I always made certain to be on hand to supervise Mr. Sinatra's selections, and to rotate his sales through the entire staff, allowing them extra commissions. (I also let them keep the sales receipts as souvenirs.)

In the early 1960s, Irving Press was a golf companion and friend of the Brioni U.S.A. representative, who was trying to open up an American market for the brand. They both contemplated a collaboration. Coincidentally, Irving was planning

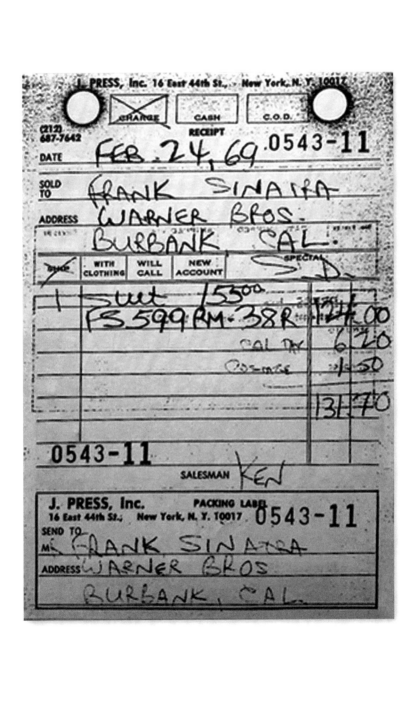

a European jaunt to include a visit to Brioni's Rome headquarters, on Via Barberini. An arrangement was made for a collection of suits and blazers in the J. Press model on Brioni patterns utilizing Italian fabrics from their top-tier Roman collection. The J. Press–Brioni collaboration featured bespoke details, including hand-sewn edges and lap seams, repp stripe/paisley silk linings, and specialty horn or brass buttons.

The venture came to an end in 1971 when Brioni expanded their American operation and their prices ballooned, dimming our early competitive advantage.

Meanwhile Ol' Blue Eyes cashed in, taking care of the Brioni remainders.

NUMBER 14

GOLDEN DAYS IN NEW HAVEN

I RECENTLY RECIEVED a note from Linda, a second cousin I grew up with in New Haven and Smith College classmate of my wife's. Her late husband and both sons are Yalies, and she felt free to throw me a curveball. "You have really recreated the Ivy League and brought it to the forefront of the J. Press world. Those of us with memories of those days and styles relish reading your words. My question, are the 'youngsters' buying the Ivy Look, or close to it? Do you feel that the look will integrate with the spectrum of today's clothes?"

Her Yale spurs brought me back to my talk several years ago at Professor Jay Gitlin's wildly popular history seminar "Yale and America." Professor Gitlin once described his class this way: "Many students want to attach themselves to that history and hook onto the legends and the traditions. I think there is still a hungering not just to know about the past but to be a part of a broader tradition."

The seminar "J. Press and Yale" later morphed into further talks at Mory's, the Elizabethan Club and Yale Bookstore, where I offered my proffer, "In Defense of Tradition." Both a duty and a pleasure to feed all those Elis the history of J. Press and how Grandpa Press founded his eponymous business at the turn of the twentieth century.

SPEAKER SERIES

RICHARD PRESS
HISTORIAN OF THE
IVY LEAGUE LOOK
GOLDEN YEARS:
IN DEFENSE OF TRADITION

WEDNESDAY, OCTOBER 16, 2013
6:00PM RECEPTION
7:00PM DINNER
$45.00 per person (inclusive)
Cancellation fee applies
Please call for reservations
203.562.3157

"Early on, I didn't know the difference between a college freshman and a senior," my grandfather expounded in a trade paper, "but I mustered up enough courage to knock on a dormitory door one afternoon. At first the boys laughed at me, but before I was through I had most of them as customers."

Unlike Grandpa, I never knocked on any student doors, just greeted them on the floor at J. Squeeze, acronym from the now deceased Fence Club. A student in the Gitlin class queried me, "Mr. Press, four years at Yale, I never owned a suit, and now I gotta dress up for interviews on Wall Street."

"Get thee to J. Press," I told him. "Choose a midweight charcoal-grey worsted suit, emblematic (maybe your Davenport College) tie, and OCBD (white cotton Oxford button-down shirt). You won't break the bank, and as a future Wall Streeter consider it a smart long-term capital investment."

Professor Gitlin was asked why students are drawn to "Yale and America." "Students don't necessarily want to be the way old Yale was," he said, "but they are curious to know what it was like and how it has changed."

Linda, so it is with J. Press, what it was like and how it's changed, but still universally tagged as "iconic purveyor of the Ivy League Look."

Riffing on "The Whiffenpoof Song":

*Gentlemen tailors off on a spree
Doomed from here to eternity,
God have mercy on such as we,
Baa, baa, baa*

NUMBER 15

MY FAVORITE PROFESSOR

PROFESSOR HERB WEST delivered his farewell address on May 28, 1964, in historic 105 Dartmouth Hall to more than a thousand students, who gave him a seven-minute standing ovation. Part of the football marching band was seated in the balcony with trumpets, tuba, and drum, ready to blare the "Dartmouth Fight Song" after the talk as if he had scored a winning touchdown.

Herbert Faulkner West was a beloved professor of comparative literature for 44 years at Dartmouth College, and I signed up for every course he offered.

Many Big Green brethren took Herb West's comp-lit classes because of their reputation as a "gut." Yet decades of students were also inspired by his keen wit and offbeat subject matter, which engaged them in works considered too avant-garde by the intellectual mainstream elite. He dissected James Joyce, T. E. Lawrence, Henry Miller, Bertolt Brecht, Christopher Isherwood, and F. Scott Fitzgerald with unsparing critical analysis.

Fellow iconoclast H. L. Mencken donated manuscript copies of his autobiography to the Dartmouth Library because of his friendship with Herb West. In late December 1940, Herb was having a drink with writer Budd Schulberg at the Hanover

Herb West was a man for all seasons.

Inn. Two years prior, Schulberg had accompanied F. Scott Fitzgerald on a trip to Hanover to work on a film script about the Dartmouth Winter Carnival. The journey turned into a drunken escapade that knocked Fitzgerald off the wagon and began his

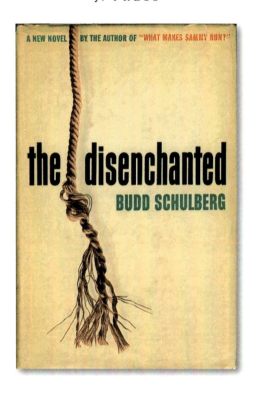

death spiral, which later served as Schulberg's inspiration for his post–World War II novel and Broadway play *The Disenchanted*. West was engaged in casual conversation with his former student when he looked up from his glass and said, "Isn't it too bad about F. Scott Fitzgerald?" This is how Schulberg learned of Fitzgerald's death.

Herb's religious skepticism is best recalled anecdotally by his son, who describes an incident that occurred with his dad's close call from a heart attack in his late forties. One day while in intensive care, he heard Father Hodder, the Hanover Episcopal priest, making his hospital rounds. Herb grabbed some lilies out of a vase, clasped them to his chest, and closed his eyes.

When Father Hodder entered the room, he took in the scene and fled.

Herb West was a man for all seasons who loved scotch and skiing. His winter advice: "Every student coming to Dartmouth should learn to ski or else miss one of the greatest advantages the college possesses." When he was a student in the winter of 1921–22, he and several classmates survived the Vale of Temp Ski Jump on a toboggan.

He dressed in nondescript wrinkled suits bought on sale at Campion's campus emporium, always fronted with a tattered L. L. Bean tartan button-down shirt and forever-stained tie. As a courtesy to me, he occasionally visited the traveling J. Press road-show exhibition upstairs from the Dartmouth Co-op. He once purchased a Dartmouth Green blazer, and I instructed the J. Press traveler to include a set of Dartmouth blazer buttons plus an Indian tie gratis. I also informed the professor that it was meant as a token of student appreciation by young Press, not as a bribe for a decent grade.

Every couple of weeks, half a dozen of my 1959 class buddies would troop to his home, several blocks south of Main Street, with a quart of Johnny Walker. We were greeted at the door by his elegant Swedish wife, whom he'd met in Weimar Berlin. Mrs. West understood her husband's predilections as she quickly departed after leading us into the thousand-edition Westholm rare-book library toting a tray of Ritz crackers, a mound of Vermont cheddar cheese, and cold veggies, with her husband comfortably ensconced in a deep leather chair awaiting our literary-locker-room binge.

Intellect, wit, and Johnny Walker so many years ago on the Hanover Plain. Dear Old Dartmouth, bless her name.

NUMBER 16

TAKING THE MEASURE OF KIM NOVAK

J. PRESS CUSTOMER Frank Sinatra famously warbled, "Regrets, I've had a few." One of my regrets to this day is that I wasn't around to fondle a tape measure around the neck of drop-dead gorgeous movie star of the day Kim Novak when she visited J. Press in 1957.

Fresh off her role as the object of Sinatra's lust and affection in the lighthearted musical *Pal Joey*, the beautiful Novak strolled in asking to see "those wonderful shirts you're famous for." Boy, would I have enjoyed being the guy whose turn it was to take that sale!

Unfortunately, the deed was done by a salesperson far more handsome than yours truly: Ray Solomon. Ray was a roustabout J. Squeeze star in our upstairs slot on the northeast corner of 44th Street and Madison Avenue. Measuring Novak up and down, he never got beyond selling her half a dozen oxford-cloth button-down shirts along with a picture in *Life* magazine.

The venture occurred when I was at Dartmouth, perambulating around the Seven Sisters (Smith, Wellesley, Vassar, etc.) in an attempt to bribe dates with Shaggy Dog sweaters. If I got past first base, perhaps, I might favor them with an OCBD like Kim Novak's. Sometimes the ruse worked, sometimes not.

The wages of sin.

NUMBER 17

THE BELLS TOLL FOR HERMAN

SIXTY-FIVE YEARS have passed since Herman the Dachshund, beloved Chi Phi (now Chi Heorot) mascot, was laid to rest in the backyard adjacent to the fraternity's parking lot before a vast, grieving Dartmouth crowd.

I was deeply honored to deliver the eulogy describing Herman's numerous contributions to the college scene. My secular rabbinic blessing, "May memories of our back-to-back, belly-to-belly signature canine stay forever within our alumni hearts."

Herman was indeed a well-known campus celebrity. He occasionally attended classes and athletic events and was often placed on the food-tray conveyor belt in Thayer Hall, the campus dining room.

The day of burial was noted in many venues throughout the college town. A fraternity brother's mother was chief librarian of Baker Library, allowing him to acquire the keys to Baker Tower and activate the sacred green tower light as well as the tower's sixteen majestic bells. Varying in size from 200 to 5,300 pounds, the bells tolled Dartmouth's alma mater across the Hanover Plain.

The pealing chimes signaled the start of a motorcade which began at the library and continued across the Dartmouth Green

THREADING THE NEEDLE II

Herman was often placed on the food-tray conveyor belt in Thayer Hall.

on East Wheelock Street to the Georgian fraternity house. An open Ford pickup truck featured the Dartmouth Indian Chiefs Dixieland Band, led by trombonist and fraternity brother Larry Elliot playing New Orleans Preservation Hall jazz funeral-cortege standards. The truck was escorted by dozens of student automobiles with lights blinking, horns blaring.

The formal social-room fraternity furniture was cleared in anticipation of the mayhem that indeed occurred as throngs of ardent mourners depleted seventeen kegs of Gansett beer that had been ordered from our local Main Street malt supplier, the Tanzi brothers.

Kindly accept my apology for my hardly Proustian "remembrance of things past." Doubt if such an event would be allowed to occur today.

The old songs, the old songs, those good old songs for me,
I love to sing those minor chords in good close harmony!

NUMBER 18

THE FORBIDDEN COLOR OF TRAD

MY RUDE AWAKENING upon joining J. Press in 1959 occurred when I dared to suggest that the company stock a black item to be as if, nothing else, a crow among the gorse, lovat, and heather-green parrots.

The only time that the "man in the gray flannel suit" of 1950s Ivy Style was ever draped in black was in the casket for his funeral. This lesson I learned at the start of my career in the family firm was imparted by Headmaster Irving Press.

One day, George Graham, top-of-the-line importer of English goods at his paisley-and-tweed-bedecked showroom on West 55th Street, was pitching Irving Press and me (an intern at the time) his world-class collection of British tie selections. Immediately, I salivated at the sight of a flamboyant yellow-and-red paisley blooming against a black ground.

"Strictly for cloak and suitors," said Uncle Irving, demeaning my choice. "Anything like it with a navy background?" he queried Mr. Graham. His suggestion birthed a J. Press standard that would rule the roost for years to come. That's how I learned to follow the boss's unbending rule—black is strictly for formal wear.

During my 35 years at J. Press, we never carried black repps or ancient madder neckties. The only exceptions; black knit ties

for yellow or pink OCBDs, black emblematic with pink pig, signature of Harvard's Porcellian Club or Yale's Fence Club tie and/or schoolboy muffler, double yellow stripes against a black ground. The Fence Club is now long gone, its remnant muffler still a Squeeze favorite, our Proustian remembrance of things past.

Twentieth-century J. Press competitors featured black Chesterfield coats, black polo shirts, black cashmere sweaters, and black informal hosiery. Chesterfield coats at J. Press held the fort via charcoal grey with only the velvet collar black. Furnishings such as scarves, sweaters, Argyle socks, Henley boating shirts, and polo shirts remained true to the Irving Press dictum, their darkest color navy blue, the mark of a gentleman.

"Anything goes" doesn't go at J. Press—especially black suits.

NUMBER 19

THE MAN IN THE 1955 IVY LEAGUE SUIT

In previous columns, I've been delighted to share memories of the Ivy heyday together with my family's history and decades at J. Press. Here's my virgin column, penned in 1955 while I was a freshman at Dartmouth. Entitled "The Ivy Look," the article appeared in DART, the school's humor magazine, and was co-authored with Art Zich, who later became a foreign correspondent for Time-Life and an associate editor of Newsweek. Pictured alongside is the original artwork that accompanied the story. Hope you enjoy it as much as we did knocking out 67 years ago with multiple cans of 'Gansett Beer.

"Who is that fellow in the Ivy League suit?" It's being whispered on campuses everywhere and not without reason. With the resurgence of conservative dress, people are finding it difficult to tell one friend from another. What's more, it's getting so that people can't even tell themselves from each other. The social implications of this situation are obvious when one considers brushing your teeth or borrowing a necktie from someone, who when you return it, turns out to be yourself.

The problem is not a new one, however, as members of the turn-of-the-century classes will admit once they have admitted they are members of the turn-of-the-century classes. The well-known "Ivy Look" had its beginnings at New Haven in the days when McKinley was president, starting the day McKinley was shot. Students usually purchased their clothing from small, modest shops, and for this reason Ivy Look tailors made little or nothing. Gradually, however, there emerged the distinctive, sophisticated attire of the Ivy Leaguer (in many ways similar to the Texas Leaguer, the Bush Leaguer, and the Real Eager, but much more distinctive, of course).

The most popular outfit in those days was the custom-tailored suit, so called because it was the custom to tailor the suit so you couldn't afford it. The custom-tailored suit gave way to the ready-made suit, which in turn gave way, but could be held together with safety-pins. Other popular "Ivy League" numbers are the Summer (summer expensive and summer cheap), the Gasuit (to be worn by people with head colds), and the bridal suite (ten dollars a night and breakfast in bed with coffee and rolls).

The first important change in the manner of Ivy Look dress after 1900 was the arrival of the "odd jacket" or sport coat, worn with "slacks," so called because of the condition of your wallet after purchasing. The "sport coat" is named after the good sports who were the first to wear it; they were later stoned to death. Today it is not uncommon to see Madison Avenue executives in the same campus tweeds that were popular during their own college days.

There are arguments concerning just what constitutes the Ivy Look. The originators are specific. Conversely, the specifiers are original. Carefully nurtured peak is the rule. The coat of the true gentleman must consist of unpadded shoulders, padded wallet, three-button high-notch lapels, and deep hook vents to let in hot and cold air. The backstrap on the trouser back is preferred, being superior to the backstrap on the trouser

"Who is the man in the Ivy League suit?"

front. The belt should be worn as high as possible, leaving none of the trouser visible above the beltline, let alone the person inside of them. Sox should be supported by garters, while garters should be supported by muscular calves. If muscular calves are not available, any form of livestock will do just as well. Shoes should be of sturdy English cut, heavy enough to keep feet out of the elements and fast enough to keep the wearer out of reach of the creditors.

Only a few varieties of shirts are permissible, and naturally, those with sleeves are preferred. The rule for college-correctness dictates button-down, round, or English tab. When confronted with the tab, it is always smarter to allow the other fellow to pick it up. The button-down demands a button on the back and pleated backs are mandatory. The wearer who has a pleated back, to begin with, is thus ahead of the game. The prescribed daytime shirt color is blue on Oxford, bowling on the Green, and drinks on the house. White is proper for evening wear unless you are spending the evening in the tub.

There is a wide choice in the selection of ties. Although some Ivy Leaguers look down on challis, a good many challis look down on Ivy Leaguers also. The exquisite foulard is always permissible, coming as it does from the French word which means "artistic fool." It goes without saying that the hard and fast rule of the Ivy Leaguer is his insistence on the four-in-hand knot. A Windsor knot, according to our sources, is strictly gauche and should only be worn by gauchos.

Dark-colored suits are the usual rule, but a clever blend of light and dark coupled with the right tie and a sheepish grin can often lend the needed sophistication, creating the illusion of correctness. When one feels he is correct enough, he may hand himself in to be marked. Brown is still the most stable color in sport coats, and also in stables.

The cloth put into the finest of the Ivy League suits is invariably imported from the British Isles. Recently the trend has been toward the importing of the British Isles. The cloth is usually produced on the antique spinning wheel of a Scotsman whose ancestors have been weaving for generations as a result of producing antique scotch.

The Ivy Look will be seen throughout the East this fall. The question remains: "Who is the man in the Ivy League suit?" It's his roommate from Exeter.

NUMBER 20

IVY LIT 101

RECENTLY I HAVE disentangled the Ivy League shelf in my bookcase. Here's the caravan that alleviated pandemic ennui.

"Your wedding day will be the second happiest day after you beat Yale," Coach tells the team in the locker room at Harvard's Memorial Stadium before the game. The John Phillips novel, *The Second Happiest Day*, isn't great literature, but if you care to stalk the heyday of Ivy in Cambridge, search out this Harvard Square creaky gem that enjoyed a brief spotlight 20 years before Yale professor Erich Segal's turgid *Love Story* soap opera, which featured the immortal line "Love means never having to say you're sorry."

Phillips's writing career was sorely tried under the paternal cloud cast by his father, Pulitzer Prize–winning author J. P. Marquand. His dad's award-winning novel, *H. M. Pulham, Esquire*, described an earlier Harvard generation and followed a townie who, not unlike the author, becomes a full-fledged Harvardian, making the best clubs and receiving the ultimate recognition: chairman of his class's 25th reunion.

F. Scott Fitzgerald admitted he'd borrowed his lead character Amory Blaine, Princeton hero of his premier novel *This Side of Paradise*, from Owen Johnson's turn-of-the-century national blockbuster, *Stover at Yale*. "My kind of textbook," Fitzgerald

F. Scott Fitzgerald

confessed. His Eli fixations—the other is Nick Carraway's *Gatsby* antagonist, Tom Buchanan—both Yalies.

Geoffrey Wolff, class of '60, updates Fitzgerald's Princeton. *The Duke of Deception: Memories of My Father* is a knowing recollection of his errant father's being tossed out of the school, a jailbird ending his life in tragic arrears. Wolff's next Old Nassau work, *The Final Club*, scripts his Seattle public-high-school protagonist with a Jewish mother and drunk father and follows him as he overcomes his negligent past to gain Princeton Eating Club acceptance (bicker), engage a Briarcliff debutante in romance, and make first-team crew on Lake Carnegie—a précis of Princeton's heyday.

Quintessential Princetonian nobility, Scott Fitzgerald self-destructs in a Shakespearean, coast-to-coast drunken binge while en route to the 1939 Dartmouth Winter Carnival in Dartmouth grad Budd Schulberg's cruelly drawn novel *The Disenchanted*, which follows the nervous breakdown he endured doing background for their movie about the Dartmouth Winter Carnival.

Beyond the comic fringe, Chris Miller, Dartmouth '62, decapitated his Hanover adventures in *The Real Animal House*, recapitulating the Alpha Delta Phi mayhem that inspired the college deconstruction that occurred during my own time at Dear Old Dartmouth. Confession: I partially shared the fabled social dysfunction at Chi Phi, my own fraternity next door.

A more significant example of the Ivy League contribution during the American Century is exemplified by the tradition of service recorded in the 1986 nonfiction work *The Wise Men: Six Friends and the World They Made*, by Walter Isaacson and Evan Thomas.

The authors elevate WASP ascendency beyond the gin-and-tonic and three-button snobbery of storied Old Money ephem era to honor the hero-ic examples of Dean Acheson, Charles E. Bohlen, W. Averell Harriman, George Kennan, Robert Lovett, and John J. McCloy, the renowned Ivy elite that delivered the Free World from both Communism and post–World War II chaos. Saviors of public service, these great men honored their Ivy academic credentials.

NUMBER 21

J. PRESS PRIME

YOU LEARN A LOT in 116 years of devotion to a single enterprise. Up to the current day, J. Press has made and fitted garments for hundreds of thousands of men. Our heritage as a custom tailor, plus our exclusive use of the finest materials, means that J. Press suits, sport coats, and trousers will fit far better "off the rack" than you might otherwise imagine. Adding to that the personal attention of skilled fitters and tailors inspires confidence in a garment that will be comfortable and flattering.

For those who desire clothing "tailored to individual order," even more benefits accrue. These include a wide selection of the world's finest fabrics and the use of only the best quality canvas, linings, trimmings, and findings. Cutting from a customer's exact measurements, the order is drafted by a highly skilled patternmaker, and careful hand-tailoring throughout the garment is accomplished by a master tailor who has devoted a lifetime to his craft. Expert fitting at the first try-on "in the rough" and at completion ensures perfect comfort and balance throughout.

The current stock at J. Press confirms the confidence shared by so many Squeeze regulars over the years. Our ties are hand-sewn from imported silks woven to our exact specifications and finished with premium linings. The full box pleat of our dress

READY TO WEAR

ALL OF OUR READY TO WEAR SUITS AND SPORT JACKETS are sold *only* at J. PRESS Stores, Travel Exhibits or by Mail Order to us and *are not obtainable elsewhere*. They conform entirely to our standards of cut and tailoring and are widely regarded as the definitive prototype for authentic conservative clothing. Except where variation is specified they are styled single breasted with three-button notch lapels, natural shoulders and steep hook vent. Trousers are slim proportioned with plain front. Some suits now include vests; where not included one can be ordered for $25.

shirts allows a comfortable fit throughout the shoulders without requiring excess fabric at the waist. The pockets on our plain-front trousers are cut on the bias, rather than vertically on the seam, for easier access and to reduce pull. Our belt loops accommodate comfortably both the traditional-width dress belt and other, wider sport belts.

J. Press Prime is reflected in the natural shoulder tailoring and high-notch lapels that provide a flattering silhouette and comfortable fit. Jacket sleeves are cut, placed, and finished with extreme care. The barrel cuff is perfectly proportioned. Jacket sleeves accommodate both barrel and French cuffs. Our jacket pockets are sewn "into" each garment, rather than "tacked" on, for a more custom look.

My first appearance on *Ivy Style*, the nostalgia-and-fashion blog, occurred several years ago in an interview with then editor in chief Christian Chensvold. He asked me the genesis of J. Press signature items. His query about hooked center vents prompted this reply:

"The fully lined steep hooked center vent assures a smoother drape, falls closed more readily and resists stretching during extended seating hours. Up until World War II, J. Press was primarily a custom tailor shop. After the war, Irving Press and Paul Press decided to manufacture ready-made suits, but knew they had to differentiate themselves from competitors. They noticed that with single-vented jackets, particularly if a guy had a big seat, the vent would separate and it was very unsightly. So they developed the hooked center vent."

Kurt Barnard, publisher of the Retail Marketing Report, was quoted in *The New York Times*, in an October 27, 1986, article, about the sale of J. Press to Kashiyama USA Inc. Referring to J. Press, he said, "They are little, yes, but they do have an impact."

Reminds me of Daniel Webster's parallel comment about my other alma mater, Dartmouth College: "It is, sir ... a small college ... Yet, there are those who love it."

RECOLLECTION

DR. JACK CARLSON

FOUNDER AND CREATIVE DIRECTOR, ROWING BLAZERS

I GREW UP *near Harvard Square, and I used to love stopping into the J. Press shop just behind the Fox Club.*

The walls were adorned with rowing blades from one of the local high schools, Browne & Nichols. And black-and-white photographs of B&N crews from the '20s, when the "Black Knights of the Charles" reigned supreme in New England rowing, defeating university crews up and down the Charles River and becoming the first American high school to win the famed Henley Royal Regatta in 1929. All of this was fascinating to me, because this was the high school I attended (and because I had the privilege of racing at Henley in 2004, on the 75th anniversary of that historic occasion).

The other decoration I recall on the walls of that venerable shop was a framed photograph of Bill Clinton being measured for a navy blazer with a big block "Y" on the pocket — which I always thought was a bit gratuitous, as everyone knows that President Clinton only attended Yale for law school, and that his real college years were spent at two other, similarly august institutions to which my own very biased preferences incline: Georgetown and Oxford.

No less captivating than the artwork (I use the term liberally) on the walls were the accessories: the belts, the watch straps, the cuff links, socks, scarves, ties, and braces. These were the real prizes for me.

Oh, and the Shaggy Dogs! The colors—and that little label with the cartoon dog—always caught my eye. One of my greatest satisfactions since starting Rowing Blazers has been collaborating with J. Press to put our own little spin on the Shaggy Dog: a limited edition with that iconic little label on the front!

NUMBER 22

THE IVY LEAGUE LOOK FOR TODAY

A RECENT BLOG posted on the estimable website *gentlemansgazette.com* featured a historical take on the "History of Preppy Style", designating J. Press as "one of the first and most iconic preppy brands.... Many believe it was J. Press that helped to shape the preppy subculture we know today."

Life magazine, in its 1954 blockbuster exposé of the genre, more accurately tagged J. Press "Home of the Ivy League Look."

The Ivy League Look was not only a wardrobe of choice owned by Ivy Leaguers. The rosters of corporate America dressed by J. Press since the 1950s "heyday of Ivy" are filled with public-high-schoolers who never heard of Hotchkiss and with non-Ivy college graduates who thought Skull and Bones was a pirate emblem.

Former Ivy Style blogger Christian Chensvold hit the mark when he wrote, "Except for a small surviving old guard, preppy has long ceased to be an expression of the culture of the elite. It is mostly divorced from the WASPY values from which it has sprung and is primarily a fashion commodity with certain social signifiers it will never shake."

When my grandfather the eponymous J. Press began his boarding-school exhibitions in the early 1900s, he didn't know

"J. Press helped to shape the preppy subculture we know today."

from "preppy." The golden rules of Jacobi Press emphasized the quality of craft, meticulous tailoring, and realistic pricing. The current purveyors bearing his name meticulously adhere to his biblical text.

Expressed in current parlance, the Ivy League Look described by *Life* magazine's 1954 article has evolved at J. Press into an anchor of restraint during an era of cultural dislocation.

The J. Press Classic Blue Blazer, single-breasted with a natural shoulder paired with our iconic OCBD (cotton Oxford button-down shirt), G.I. khaki, or poplin trousers (displayed in an encyclopedic variety of colors at J. Press) is our non-kitschy office stand-in for the formerly sacrosanct business suit.

Times have changed, but Grandpa's decree of quality, craft, and meticulous tailoring paired with realistic pricing remains extant in the 117-year-old headquarters bearing his name.

NUMBER 23

WITH POPPY BUSH AND BABE RUTH

THE NEW BASEBALL SEASON hovers on the horizon, and memories of my brief time at Yale Field with "Poppy" Bush and Babe Ruth make my heart beat faster every April.

Destiny and Power, Jon Meacham's surprisingly vivid biography of former president George H. W. Bush, is Shakespearean in its depiction of family, power, and public service. It also briefly describes an incident from one of the great days in the life of 10-year-old Richard Press.

My beloved uncle, the state senator and New Haven City Court judge Harold E. Alprovis, was a 1948 political crony of then Connecticut Republican finance chairman and, later, U.S. senator Prescott Bush. He invited my uncle with me in tow, along with a gaggle of politicians to the Princeton baseball game at Yale Field. It was also the day Babe Ruth came to New Haven to gift his memoirs to Yale.

Prescott's son, George H. W., familiarly tagged as "Poppy," was the first baseman and captain of the Yale team. He accepted the manuscript from Ruth at a temporary microphone set up on the pitcher's mound. It had rained all morning, but with Babe's appearance, the sun came out. Ruth was already frail, stricken with cancer that would kill him three months later.

The bleachers were loaded with local kids, many of them

Babe Ruth meets George H. W. "Poppy" Bush.

my fifth-grade classmates at Beecher School. Republican mayor William Celentano, part of our crowd, presented Ruth with a certificate proclaiming lifetime membership in New Haven Little League. Deeply moved, Ruth responded, croaking tortured words into the microphone. After the ceremony, he donned a cream-colored Ascot cap, and the politicos fittingly seated him next to 10-year-old Richard Press, right on the first-base line. He kindly signed my program before leaving after a few innings.

After the game (which Yale won), Mr. Bush introduced us to his son Poppy, who autographed my program right underneath Babe Ruth's signature, a misbegotten treasure lost to the ages.

Meacham's treatise recalled Poppy's early married years in New Haven, a G.I. war hero gallantly completing his Phi Beta Kappa Yale degree in two and a half years. Paul Press, obsessive raconteur of celebrities he'd befriended in and around his York Street store, recalled the era in a magazine interview: "Poppy Bush was a very nice man," my dad exclaimed. "In the 40s his wife, Barbara, was working at the Yale Co-op on York Street. I ran into her so often that she teased me I never invite her for lunch."

When Bush was running for vice president in 1980, he gave a speech on the Yale campus that was interrupted by a heckler who accused him of being a "Brooks Brothers Republican." Bush opened up his jacket, revealing his suit was actually by J. Press. None of us Presses, nor any of the sales staff, remember his patronage. Biographer Meacham clarifies the issue, noting "his suits (42 long, 38 waist) came from Washington clothier Arthur A. Adler; his shirts (which Bush, in a phrase that betrayed his Greenwich origins, called "shirting" in private) from Ascot Chang, a Hong Kong tailor."

Nowadays, the presidency of George H. W. Bush can be comfortably digested, perhaps even by Democrats, distributing triumph and disappointment of times past. H.W. never regretted articulating the famous credo that cost him his job:

"Read my lips."

NUMBER 24

WHITE DUCKS VS. KHAKI CHINOS

MY LONGTIME INSTALLATION in the family business occurred during the tragically short period of the Camelot-J.F.K. era. During that time, 44th Street was a manifest of the Kennedy ethos. The Kennedy white duck–khaki chino affection reflects the J. Press bespoke-white-flannel-trouser custom promoted by my eponymous grandfather at the turn of the twentieth century to complement the blue-blazer outfit that was customary for weekend or resort wear.

Ambassador Joe Kennedy Sr. preferred his white trousers in a more formal royal-British mode, expressed by fine-twilled gabardine worsted trousers. To meet the match, J. Press provides an enlarged choice, tailored to individual order for those favoring white or cream lightweight wool flannels, tropical worsteds, or classic linens.

Archival Kennedy pictures illustrate the family penchant for white ducks and khaki chinos. Papa Joe, Jack, and brother Joe junior appeared in 1930s Palm Beach sporting white ducks anchored by matching brown-and-white Oxford full brogue saddle shoes.

The Kennedy era captured Jack and Bobby in Hyannis Port wearing sport jackets over white cotton ducks. President Kennedy dons a sport coat and khaki chinos as he chats with

THREADING THE NEEDLE II

JFK in khakis.

Defense Secretary Robert McNamara. J.F.K. throws a touchdown pass to his brother Bobby, both of them in chinos.

J. Press presents a post-Kennedy collection of plain-front khaki chinos. First worn on college campuses by ex-servicemen following passage of the G.I. Bill of Rights and quickly adopted by students across the country, cotton khaki trousers remain a pillar of the heyday of the Ivy League Look. Escalating the choice of white ducks vs. khaki chinos, J. Press offers our washed twill, 100 percent cotton trousers in light khaki and classic white.

A Hyannis Port invite isn't required for the purchase.

NUMBER 25

STEALING THE HARVARD DRUM

A HUMOROUS MEMORY of a fraternity football-season shenanigan not otherwise portrayed in the campus satire *Animal House* inspired by my dear old Dartmouth. The 1957 Harvard Drum Riot I spectated didn't make the silver screen, so here's my eyewitness account.

Coach Bob Blackman's Dartmouth Indians (another blasphemy from earlier times) were creaming Harvard 26–0 going into halftime. *The Harvard Crimson* reported the ensuing brouhaha:

Dartmouth students always try to get at least a piece of the big drum and when it returned from repairs in the Midwest in 1957, they especially wanted it. As the members of the Harvard Band faced the home stands and played "Let Me Call You Sweetheart," some Dartmouth fraternity pledges attacked the drum guards. The musicians turned around, were insulted to see the big drum being threatened, and ran to defend it. A halftime jam ensued with about 500 students throwing body-blocks and punches, but the musicians finally beat off their attackers with their instruments. The fruit was borne shortly thereafter in Hanover when eight fraternities, including my own beloved Chi Phi, were placed on probation for the rest of the semester. The action was taken by the Committee on Administration as punishment for the halftime fracas caused by fraternity pledges. The eight fraternities, comprising about 520 young men, were forbidden to hold any parties on or off campus, or to have women or liquor in the houses. The penalties, the harshest during my time in Hanover, were announced in a special decision by the faculty committee.

The Harvard Crimson offered further editorial comment, noting that, in overthrowing the milder punishments recommended by the Inter-fraternity Judiciary Committee, the faculty group stated that the pledges of the eight fraternities had "degraded themselves, their fraternities and their college."

The decision was met with valor by my frat brethren when we unanimously decided punishment was to be celebrated every night of the remaining semester by downing kegs of beer. The kegs were delivered to the house each afternoon by reliable Tanzi Brothers Market, regular campus suppliers of malt hooch. The so-called prohibition of liquor had failed to specify beer.

I returned home for Christmas vacation with my size-33 waist having expanded to a very tight size 36. This column is not meant to be an apologia. Times have changed, and we've often rewound the clock since the Puritans landed on Plymouth Rock.

The fraternity system at Dartmouth is on the way out, but when I returned for my 50th reunion, there still remained on the dilapidated basement-barroom wall our honorarium bronze plaque:

Never have so many given so much for so little.

We decided punishment was to be celebrated every night of the remaining semester by downing kegs of beer.

NUMBER 26

YORK STREET SPREZZATURA

FOLLOWING the golden rule of Renaissance courtier Baldassar Castiglione, Paul Press defined J. Press sprezzatura as a certain nonchalance so as to conceal all art and make whatever one does appear to be without effort or thought. And so it was with his own personal wardrobe.

Since his years at New Haven Hillhouse High School (suitably attired varsity-basketball manager), his forgiving father enabled his addiction to bespoke tailoring and imported British haberdashery, always anchored by Lobb shoes or Gucci leather horsebit loafers. In his college years during the Depression, he sported his unlikely wardrobe at the decidedly non-Ivy campus of the University of Pittsburgh, at the time bestraught by the city's teeming smokestacks. During baseball season, he spent much of his time at nearby Forbes Field, cheering on the Pittsburgh Pirates, a lifelong obsession paired with his Duke of Windsor wardrobe, home, and office caches of Upmann cigars and decades of country-club tournament tennis.

Tagged as "the Cary Grant of 262 York Street," Paul Press ruled the sartorial roost from his office headquarters overlooking Yale's Branford College. Family pictures left in his desk after the 1986 sale of the business to Onward Kashiyama were kindly handed over to yours truly by the new owners.

"The Cary Grant of 262 York Street."

J. PRESS

The collection also included him with Mom in St. Mark's Square and my intergenerational favorite, at age 90, four years before his death in 2005, arm around great-grandson Samuel Press Goodkind, now a Los Angeles associate at a preeminent design-management agency.

My father displays his singular version of a "buttonless button-down" shirt. Tailored for him by J. Press shirtmaker Troy Guild in the 1960s, the shirt features a contrast white broadcloth point collar, miming the standard J. Press button-down, with French cuffs on a blue end-on-end madras body made of 100 percent fine-spun cotton. He achieved the curled-collar look of the button-down simply by removing the stays underneath the collar. His sport coat, 1971 J. Press bespoke made of luxurious 100 percent cashmere from W. Bill, London.

A sprezzatura man for all seasons.

NUMBER 27

HEYDAY OF THE IVY LEAGUE SUIT

THE HIGH-WATER MARK of the Ivy League suit in America coincided with the Kennedy years. J. Press opened its first street-level New York store at 16 East 44th Street during the high times of Camelot. Nobody who was anybody was clad in anything but a natural shoulder suit.

During my salad days in the family business, all of America wore suits. Our genre was one of a kind. The J. Press style was copied throughout department stores and Main Street specialty stores from coast to coast. Few J. Press competitors matched the munificent natural-shoulder selection tailored to our unique requirements. All of our ready-to-wear suits and sport jackets were standard in cut and tailoring, with single-breasted three-button front, high-notch lapel, natural shoulder, and steep center hook vent. Trousers were plain front, slim cut, and featured a 20-inch knee and a 17-inch bottom.

The two thousand suits hanging on the racks at the 44th Street store fell into 10 categories. Textbook breakdown: milled-worsted Glenurquharts, clear-cut pure-wool worsteds, British six-ply lattice-weave worsteds, Saxony-worsted Glens, striped worsteds, flannel-finish pure worsteds, milled-worsted herringbone, worsted twists, British Saxony worsted-tweed herringbones, narrow and thick wale combed-cotton corduroy, and Cheviot worsted-tweed herringbones.

J. PRESS

The high-water mark of the Ivy League suit in America coincided with the Kennedy years.

Further illustrating the perennial vogue for past and present classics, best-selling striped worsteds were available in muted, one-eighth-inch pinstripe in deep blue, in muted quarter-inch pinstripe, in unfinished worsted in midnight grey, and in top-of-the-line muted half-inch chalk-stripe flannel-finish worsted in dark grey or dark blue.

The Man in the Gray Flannel Suit, beyond the famous Gregory Peck cinematic portrayal, nevertheless retained its 1950s popularity, justly regarded by the well-groomed cognoscenti of the times as the all-purpose indispensable look. Plain shades of Oxford grey and clerical grey were standard fare.

Never to forget whipcord twists in tan mixtures that several years later were Frank Sinatra's favorite, he purchased in bulk. Cheviot tweeds remained popular remnants from J. Press campus stores at

Yale and Harvard. Singular in their stereotypical campus appeal via their rugged resilience and unusual colorings in Moorish shades of lovat, heather, clerical grey, bracken, and black briar brown Hollywood-ready paired with New Haven Owl Shop bulldog pipes.

The target J. Press customer in the heyday of Ivy had at least five suits in his wardrobe requiring significant replacement every fall season. We offered both newcomers and our hardy clientele an encyclopedia of choices.

Let the suit trumpets roar once more.

NUMBER 28

THE BOSS CHATS WITH OL' BLUE EYES

IRVING PRESS was an unusual boss. Not many men's clothiers are graduates of Yale Law School, and few if any hang out regularly at the Yale Club on Vanderbilt and 44th Street, which, nearly three decades after his passing, bestrides the flagship store of the company he once headed.

His wide interests and circle of friends ranged from golf cohorts, Yale intimates, Scottish Mill tradesmen, menswear mavens, and many of the J. Press customers whom he ended up conversing with under the bolts of woolens in his favored corner by the customs department.

Frank Sinatra's time at J. Press in 1969 included many visits to 16 East 44th Street, where he got to know most of the staff on a first-name basis, generously signing autographs for whoever had the nerve to ask him.

Uncle Irving Press and Frank happened to bond one day after I introduced them. They engaged one another in discussions of Sinatra's boyhood idol and my uncle's classmate, the singer and entertainer Rudy Vallee. Known as "America's Crooner" several years before Bing Crosby's hit records and more than a decade before Sinatra's, Vallee transferred from the University of Maine to join my uncle in the Yale class of 1926.

The men were also members of the Yale Collegians, a band

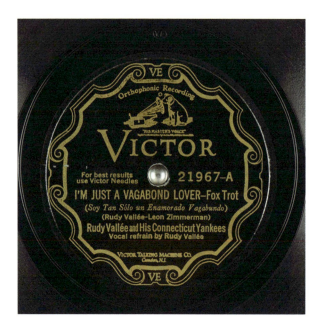

made up of students working their way through college by both playing music in the student dining hall in exchange for free meals and by taking on paying gigs at country clubs, school dances, and proms. Sinatra particularly liked Irving's story about how, when a singing violinist didn't work out (and they rarely do!), Vallee began singing through the same megaphone he'd used to project the volume of his saxophone, alongside non-singing violinist Uncle Irving, who regularly shared the stage with him.

But when Rudy packed up the Collegians (along with his degree in philosophy) and they took up residence as the house band at the Heigh-Ho Club at 35 East 53rd Street in Manhattan, neither of his two violinists was named Irving Press. It was a personnel decision that would forever alter the history of both popular music and men's clothing.

NUMBER 29

TIME MARCHES ON

AMERICA'S ROMANCE with Yale first blossomed in 1901, when senior Alan Hirsch copyrighted his rousing football song "Boola Boola," which sold more sheet music the following year than any other song. It became so popular that John Philip Sousa performed it alongside "The Stars and Stripes Forever." The country's favorite ragtime duo, Irene and Vernon Castle, performed "Boola Boola" as a turkey trot.

It hit the charts the same time that Burt Standish's frolicsome *Frank Merriwell at Yale* became a dime-novel best-seller in Main Street drugstores. It also evolved into comic books, ending the 1940s as a popular NBC radio show. Hicks in the sticks voted Frank Merriwell the original all-American boy.

Then another roar, louder, wilder, louder, full of unbounded joy. The Yale cheer! The band drowned out by all the uproar. The sight of sturdy lads in blue, delicious with delight, hugging a dust-covered youth, lifting him to their shoulders and bearing him away in triumph. Merriwell had won his own game, and his record was made. It was a glorious finish. Old Yale can't get along without him.

Soon Scribner's on Fifth Avenue upended the dime-novel heroics of Merriwell and stocked the upscale shelves with Owen Johnson's *Dink Stover at Yale*, the 1912 blockbuster that F. Scott Fitzgerald famously acknowledged as the textbook of his generation. The book's dramatic crisis resolved with Dink tapped for Skull and Bones:

THREADING THE NEEDLE II

I am not satisfied with Yale as a magnificent factory on democratic business lines, I dream of something else, something visionary, a great institution not of boys, clean, lovable and honest, but of men of brains, of courage, of leadership, a great center of thought to stir the country.

In 1954, magazine magnate Henry Luce, Yale '20, OK'd the article that appeared in *Life* magazine and was devoured by 10 million readers. "The Ivy Look Heads Across the US" pinpointed New Haven as the look's home. "Sometimes regarded more of a club than a clothes shop," the article said, "J. Press is delighted that its look is now capturing the country." *Life* also benignly credits Brooks Brothers as "perpetuating the Madison Avenue look."

Brooks Brothers never deigned to open a store in New Haven. Playing Second Hand Rose, the company tendered biweekly retail travel exhibits in the Hotel Taft. With J. Press at the top of the pack, local merchants including Arthur Rosenberg, Fenn-Feinstein, White's, and Langrock bended their knees to the nascent aristocracy, who paid for their wares with proceeds from the family trust.

A virulent fever erupted in the 60s, forever changing Old Eli. Co-education, anti-war protests, and civil-rights riots threw the New Haven heyday of Ivy into the dustbin of history.

"Where'er upon life's seas we sail, for God, for Country and for Yale" is still audible in Battell Chapel as in days of old now charged with a changing cast that sings to the song of a different drummer.

Henry Luce's twentieth-century newsreel banner hits the right note for postmodern twenty-first-century Yale …

TIME MARCHES ON.

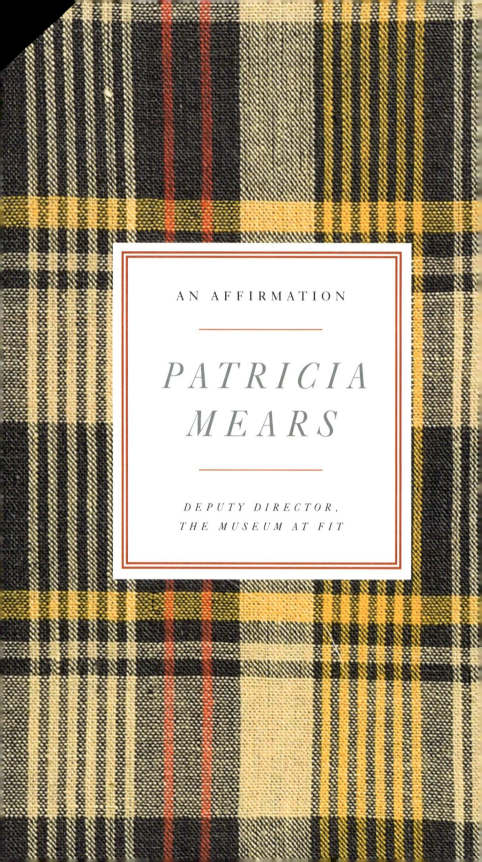

AN AFFIRMATION

PATRICIA MEARS

DEPUTY DIRECTOR,
THE MUSEUM AT FIT

AS A CURATOR *who has organized a couple of dozen exhibitions, I am inevitably asked the same question: What is your favorite object in the show? In "Ballerina," it was Anna Pavlova's Dying Swan costume; in "Expedition," it was a fur parka worn by African-American explorer Matthew Henson.*

In the 2012 Ivy Style exhibition, it was a trio of tweed jackets Richard Press lent to the museum. Ivy connoisseurs can readily see they are wonderful examples of the genre as they are beautifully tailored and made with the finest fabrics. For me, however, they transcended mere quality. The jackets, poignant and compelling beyond their materiality, belonged to his beloved father, Paul. Richard, half-jokingly, told me they may need conservation because of the many tears he spilled on them in the decades since his father's passing.

Richard's comment affirmed what I felt from the moment I met him. Beyond his expertise and utter charm, Richard Press's best quality is his profound humanity. He is a mensch, a wonderful Yiddish word meaning a person of great honor and integrity. How lucky was I to have Richard, along with G. Bruce Boyer, be my Ivy Style partner and guide?

NUMBER 30

BELOW NOB HILL

MY FAVORITE San Francisco happenings occurred from 1968 through 1980 below Nob Hill. In 1968, Jack Kennedy, the J. Press West Coast sales rep, moved from his showings at the Clift Hotel to managing our new store at 411 Post Street, directly across from Gump's legendary department store. Featuring high-end gifts, housewares, and jewelry synonymous with San Francisco in its elegance, Gump's had a worldly style and maverick spirit that provided a good fit for J. Press.

A well-appointed, street-level window display of Ivy Style heyday fronted the elegant lobby, with its private elevator to the second-floor shop. Irving Press, Yale, '26, designed the store, replicating the Eli look of Davenport College's lounge adjacent to our home store. Nudging nearby Brooks Brothers and Cable Car Clothiers, the Press boys offered unique York Street, New Haven, ambiance to Bohemian Club cognoscenti campus, adding authenticity for Stanford University with nary an equivalent in Palo Alto.

Jack Kennedy's Irish bonhomie personalized the San Francisco store's panache. After graduating from Hillhouse High, Kennedy started his retail career by selling white bucks at Barrie Ltd., the legendary shoe store located right beside J. Press in New Haven. He ingratiated himself with his role

411 Post Street, directly across from Gump's legendary department store

model, Paul Press, and my dad immediately spotted rookie talent, offering him a job next door. An opening on the J. Press West Coast route occurred when the current rep deserted the company to join a New Haven competitor. Kennedy quickly filled the void, connecting with the former rep's fans. Many of the top-tier Nob Hill crowd lobbied the Press boys—Irving, Paul, and yours truly—to open a San Francisco branch with Kennedy as its manager. The shotgun wedding took place shortly thereafter.

Local celebrity Barnaby Conrad enhanced the connection. Conrad was an American artist, author, nightclub proprietor, bullfighter, and boxer. Born in San Francisco to an affluent family, he was sent east to prep at the Taft School in Watertown, Connecticut, and attended Yale, studying painting circa 1943.

J. PRESS

A man for all seasons, he opened the El Matador nightclub in 1953. Conrad was a J. Press aficionado since his time at Taft and Yale, and his bistro became San Francisco's version of the New York City Stork Club for local elites to meet, eat, and greet.

Local bon vivant Norman Hobman, or "Henry Africa" as he was also known, opened the Dartmouth Social Club in the Marina on the corner of Greenwich and Fillmore. Capitalizing on the nascent *Preppy Handbook* craze, he recruited genuine Dartmouth graduates to man the bar in white button-downs, aprons, and knit ties. Dick Press tippled and sang many Big Green songs at the bar.

In 1980, we were about to lose the lease on the store. Kennedy wanted to move back to New Haven and renew family ties. We felt that our personnel resources were strained, and rather than find a new lease, we decided to move Kennedy back to the New Haven store to replace my father, who was getting older. It was sensible under these circumstances not to move forward with further investment in San Francisco. It had been successful and profitable, but, expressing prudence over pride, we decided to leave on that note.

I left my heart in San Francisco, along with plenty of empty highball glasses at El Matador and the Dartmouth Social Club.

NUMBER 31

THE 2000-YEAR-OLD MAN ON 44TH STREET

READING MEL BROOKS'S recent book, *All About Me*, brought to mind my hysterical weeping years ago upon first hearing his LP record *The 2000 Year Old Man*, a multitude of comedy sketches he performed with Carl Reiner.

The Press boys, Uncle Irving and Papa Paul, unknowingly echoed the Brooks-Reiner routine—minus the Yiddish accents.

The Brooks-Reiner version:

> REINER: *Oh, boy. You knew Jesus?*
>
> BROOKS: *Yeah. Thin lad, wore sandals, long hair, walked around with 11 other guys. Always came into the store, never bought anything. Always asked for water.*

The heyday shop at 16 East 44th Street had a private telephone line from Uncle Irving's private corner in the custom department to Dad's office in New Haven. I remember once taking the phone from my uncle:

"Dad, Prince Albert of Monaco, Grace Kelly's son, just came into the store with a retinue of retainers all decked out in Paul Stuart. Never bought anything."

Mel Brooks, the 2000 Year Old Man, with Carl Reiner.

Irving frequently one-upped his brother by bragging to him about the vast coterie of top-tier celebrities he'd befriended who "came into the store and bought." Dad's purview was strictly New Haven, albeit patrician bands of Elis renewing their patronage and friendship with Paul Press often cited by them, "the Cary Grant of York Street."

New York social climber Dick Press utilized club memberships, charity benefits, prep-school and college reunions, and top-echelon boozing all over town to lure these tribal entities into J. Squeeze. Unlike in the Jesus/Two Thousand Year Old Man chatter, none of them wore sandals or sported long hair. Most of them bought. And they didn't ask for water.

Back to Mel Brooks: *"Tragedy is when I cut my finger. Comedy is when you walk into an open sewer and die."*

I walked into plenty of open sewers during my years on 44th Street; however, I'm still breathing.

NUMBER 32

CYNOSURE OF AMERICAN STYLE

SINCE 1915, the Brooks Brothers headquarters stood entrenched at 346 Madison Avenue, the Rock of Gibraltar, warp and woof of Establishment power. Brooks Brothers even motivated my grandfather, the eponymous J. Press, to march me across Madison Avenue from his second-floor shop to their boys' department for my Bar Mitzvah suit some seventy years ago. The salesmen on the first floor knew him well, bowing to him as if he were royalty. Soon after I tried on my boy's size-14 grey flannel suit, he paid for it in cash, trooping back to his shop across the street, where he tore off the offending label and affixed his signature one in place. Grandpa proceeded to pin and chalk the suit in preparation for my fashionable Torah presentation at the altar of Temple Mishkan Israel.

The turn-of-the-20th-century New Haven retailers all borrowed the Brooks No. 1 sack suit and button-down collar shirts, with David Langrock, Bill Fenn, his brother Jack Feinstein, Arthur Rosenberg, Izzy White, Sam Rosenthal, and Moe Maretz all "following suit." Grandpa enlarged the Brooks apocrypha to redefine his own version with a flap pocket on the OCBDs and raised notch lapels on suit jackets, sport coats, and blazers—all with signature center hook vents.

J. PRESS

Recalling his days at Yale, former Episcopal Archbishop of New York Paul Moore Jr., in the memoir *My Harvard, My Yale*, credited Jacobi Press with doing more than anyone else to establish the Ivy Look. "His tweeds were a little softer and flashier than Brooks Brothers tweed," Moore writes, "his ties a little brighter."

Manufacturers and retailers nationwide got in on the act, including manufacturers Gant and Sero Shirt Makers in New Haven; Hathaway Shirts in Waterville, Maine; Troy Guild in upstate New York; and suit-makers Norman Hilton, Julie Hertling, Hickey Freeman, Linett, H. Freeman, Haspel Brothers, and Gordon-Ford.

Life magazine, nevertheless, recognized the J. Press campus stores along with urban Brooks Brothers as progenitors of the Ivy League Look. The article heralded its 1954 coast-to-coast implosion by Main Street retailers.

Today, J. Press expands 21st-century resources to rejuvenate popular styles honed during its long and illustrious history, currently serving the day-to-day and weekend requirements of both our in-store and online clientele.

One block east of the now skeletal Rock of Gibraltar, side by side with the Yale Club, together with our New Haven and Washington, D.C., shops, J. Press proudly retains the crown—Cynosure of American Style.

NUMBER 33

POLO SHIRT SPREZZATURA

IN 2013, the blizzard Nemo literally brought down the roof of the historic J. Press headquarters at 262 York Street. A framed picture of my dad, Paul Press, in tennis gear on the courts at the Caribe Hilton hotel, in San Juan, Puerto Rico, in 1954, with Wimbledon great Fred Perry hung in a place of honor at the back of the store in the prime fitting room. They crossed racquets over the net clad in Mr. Perry's eponymous tennis whites that were confined to the J. Press geographic U.S. locales at that time.

After the brand went national, Fred Perry and J. Press parted racquets. No longer did laurel wreaths adorn Squeeze polo shirts. Nor will you find polo mallets, alligators, frogs, hanging sheep, whales, or any other accoutrements of the national brands. Avid polo lover Winston Churchill once remarked, "A polo handicap is a person's ticket to the world." J. Press chukka polo shirts play the game clean and straight.

Ennobling our historic plain-front polos, an abundance of trad colors are enlarged beyond tennis white in a merry-go-round of hues. A rejuvenated old-time favorite is our distinct solid Jersey button-down short-sleeve polo enhanced by our J. Press button-flap breast pocket in classic colors.

J. PRESS

J. Press polo shirts play the game clean and straight.

Ideal for comfortable weekend or casual business wear, our striped polos feature a cornucopia of combinations.

J. Press polo shirts define sprezzatura with either a blazer, khakis, poplins, grey tropicals, or Bermuda shorts. Baldassare Castiglione—Italian courtier, diplomat, soldier, and prominent Renaissance author—defined the term 500 years ago.

Practice in everything a certain nonchalance
That shall conceal design and show
That what is done and said is done without effort
And almost without thought.

NUMBER 34

LORD ATTLEE MEETS DICK PRESS

DURING MY SENIOR YEAR at Dartmouth, in the winter of 1959, there occurred an unlikely scotch-whiskey joust with Lord Attlee, former prime minister of England.

Clement Attlee memorably defeated Prime Minister Winston Churchill in a landslide election in June 1945, taking his place at the same time as President Harry S. Truman and Soviet premier Joseph Stalin's meeting at the Potsdam Conference. Following his retirement from politics, Attlee was elevated to the peerage, taking his seat in the House of Lords in 1955.

For reasons unknown—perhaps my perceived joie de vivre—I was selected to be a member of the Welcoming Committee for the Great Issues Class, a senior-curriculum subject.

The Great Issues course brought to campus a weekly series of illustrious speakers to educate seniors on pressing national and international issues of the time. Speakers included Robert Frost (class of 1896), former secretary of state Dean Acheson, Supreme Court justice Thurgood Marshall, containment strategist George Kennan, New York governor Nelson Rockefeller (class of 1930), and conservative commentator William F. Buckley Jr.

My assignment on a bleak snowy winter afternoon was to pick up Lord Attlee at the nearby White River Junction, Vermont railroad station, where he was expected to arrive from Boston. I was to transport him back to Hanover. The conveyance was my battered 1954 Chevrolet Bel Air, veteran of numerous fraternity road trips to Smith and Skidmore, nicknamed "Sheldon Chevrolet" and always parked in the back lot of my Chi Phi fraternity.

As Lord Attlee arrived at the primitive White River Junction station, he emerged quite alone, introducing himself to me as if I were but a hired retainer. Holding a note telling him that a student, Richard Press, would meet him when he arrived, I retrieved his two pieces of Louis Vuitton luggage, which barely fit in the rear trunk along with the proverbial spare tire.

"Mr. Press, my ungodly journey from North Station on an unspeakable turn-of-the-century train car requires me to take whiskey refreshment. Kindly take me to wherever we might find immediate relief. I would most certainly enjoy your company elucidating your own Dartmouth College experience."

Twenty minutes later we were seated at the cocktail lounge of the Hanover Inn, normally not a student domain. Lord Attlee ordered the lounge attendant, who gaped, open-mouthed, in apparent trauma: "Two double scotch whiskeys for each of us."

Lord Attlee was wearing a three-piece charcoal-grey, striped-herringbone suit that I assumed was tailored on Savile Row. I was draped in my sole Dartmouth suit, a J. Press charcoal-grey, striped-herringbone Huddersfield suit not unlike his.

After our first round, Lord Attlee complimented my wardrobe. Three sheets to the wind, I regaled him about J. Press and my family history. Well into the hour and maybe our third round, two faculty members originally delegated to meet him in the hotel lounge were belatedly informed of our presence in

"Kindly take me to wherever we might find immediate relief."

the cocktail lounge. They rushed in greeting him and angrily shooing me away. Noting my condition, one of them threatened me with dire consequences. Lord Attlee, aware of my possible indictment, informed them that he'd enjoyed the pleasure of my company and being fed much Dartmouth information.

He whispered to me, "Mr. Press, these faculty members are rather shabbily attired, unlike yourself." I was already plastered while he bid me a hearty farewell, himself straight as an arrow. Shortly thereafter, I sat amongst my classmates in 105 Dartmouth Hall to hear his talk. After the fleeting introduction, I passed out in my seat, only to be awakened during the applause.

For he himself has said it,
And it's greatly to his credit,
That he is an Englishman!

NUMBER 35

FIGHT FIERCELY AT HARVARD

MEMORIES OF OUR LATE and lamented Cambridge store are ever present in my mind. I recently discovered the sidebar picture of the Cambridge staff in the late 1980s, which further fanned the flame.

Be still heart—a recent note (edited) from a Crimson loyalist:

A good friend of mine, an Eli who is dismissive of my two Harvard degrees, sent me some of your articles about J. Press and related items. Am a lifelong fan and would like to tell you how I joined up. Prior to enlisting in the Navy, I spent 4 years at an Episcopal military academy.

I wore uniforms there and in the Navy. Thus, when I arrived in Cambridge my civilian attire was thin. I also observed that wasn't what was being worn around the Yard. I asked where did one go to get outfitted and I was told J. August and J. Press in Harvard Square and Brooks Bros in Boston. I first went to the J. Press store which was on the first floor of the D U Club. I was very impressed and went in.

J. PRESS

A very knowledgeable salesman took me in hand and I soon found myself acquiring a de rigueur wardrobe consisting of grey flannel trousers, a Harris Tweed "odd" jacket, white button-down shirts, repp ties, argyle socks, penny loafers and a light wool topcoat. The salesman said I would need formal wear for all the debutante balls I would be attending so next was a tuxedo with dancing pumps adorned with silk bows and a dark wool overcoat called a Chesterfield. Finally, he said I should have a Tattersall Vest. I'd never heard of such an animal much less seen one in Oklahoma but when he brought out this beautiful blue and black checkered vest I fell in love with the vest and J. Press. I remained a loyal customer for my six years at Harvard. What a great store and what wonderful people worked there!

All eighty-plus years at the corner of Dunster and Mt. Auburn have hardly come to naught. My personal highlight is the recollection longtime manager Al Goro fed me about his times selling, fitting, and conversing with poet Robert Frost, enabling his collection of Donegal and Harris Tweed suits.

The Harvard Gazette, in a 2016 article fittingly titled "Style with Staying Power," quotes an observer from the class of '58: "J. Press had the most exclusive reputation of the clothing shops in Harvard Square during his era. Harvard students could generally recognize a J. Press suit on a man as opposed to a Coop or Brooks Brothers suit. I don't know how we knew but we did."

My favorite nugget: "Harvard lecturer Stephen Shoemaker, whose courses include Harvard's History and Evolving Religious Identity, has been a J. Press customer since the 1990s. His students often ask him why he always has to dress up for class. To which Shoemaker, in his three-piece suit, is often tempted to

respond: "Well, why do you always have to dress so down for class?"

Menswear brick-and-mortar remains in uncertain times. Harvard contributes to retail uncertainty around the Square with real-estate ventures at a standstill. The times they are a-changin'. The iconic newsstand in the heart of Harvard Square shuttered its panels and emptied its stands for good.

Bystanders report the old J. Press space in the former D.U. Club a ghostlike remnant, with local gossip suggesting a bistro somehow somewhere.

J. Squeeze returning to the hood? Songster and satirist Tom Lehrer's undying lyric may or may not foresee the future:

> *Fight fiercely, Harvard ... Albeit they possess the might,*
> *Nonetheless we have the will.*

MUSINGS

SCOTT HILL

*CREATIVE DIRECTOR,
AMERICAN FOLKWAYS*

J. PRESS *is not only upright and breathing after more than a century, it is on the move ... with a tight spring in its step. Clearly the Press diet of steady, thoughtful style moderation, beautiful cloth, and adherence to focused and stellar customer service is key to its supple arterial clarity and hearty longevity in the sartorial "blue zone." I like to call Press the "Mothership," the Source, the Headwaters, the Magic World Ash, the very center of the mandala ... the Axis Mundi of "That Much Sought-After Look." It is the place of comfort, curiosity, collegial goodwill, fellowship, and modest good-looking clothing. I am thrilled to be able to contribute whatever small part I can offer to this seminal and noble brand. It is and will continue to be American bedrock, an island unto itself where generations can live safely and be fortified with the strong grain of style and tradition.*

John Chancellor, anchorman.

NUMBER 36

WITH JOHN CHANCELLOR AT THE SUMMIT

JOHN CHANCELLOR served as anchor of the *NBC Nightly News* from 1970 to 1982. He was a dedicated J. Press customer from the early 1960s until his death, in 1996. I was with him shortly after his arrest at the 1964 Republican National Convention for refusing to cede his spot on the floor to the "Goldwater Girls," supporters of the Republican presidential candidate. "How about fitting a jailbird, Richard?" he said to me.

A family entanglement with John Chancellor occurred at the 1985 Reagan-Gorbachev summit in Geneva. Before the trip, when Chancellor told me about his summit assignment, I told him my son Ben was spending his freshman fall semester at Franklin College in Lugano prior to entering Middlebury. "Tell him to call me," Chancellor responded. "I'll show him around." Here's my son's version of the ensuing event:

Chancellor was a very kind, approachable and authentic man. He reminded me more of one of my prep-school teachers than an anchor of the leading American network's evening news broadcast.

After Chancellor's personally guided tour, he said it'd be necessary for me to secure a press-pass badge in order to be allowed in proximity to the briefings from the White House press secretary at Geneva's Hall of Justice, near NBC's headquarters. Chancellor placed himself behind a secretary's typewriter on the spot and began typing away at a letter on NBC News letterhead attesting to my being editor in chief of The Franklin College Tribune. He endorsed me in the letter and signed it as well. I closely followed his instructions to take the "letter of accreditation" to Switzerland's Accreditation Bureau a few blocks away.

Arriving at the pickup desk, a Swiss security official bluntly stated to me the letter was a fake, he knew I was not editor of the college newspaper (Franklin didn't have a newspaper!), and he'd spoken with Franklin's dean, who said he would immediately handle the ensuing punitive disciplinary action which was, he informed me, fortunate, since fraud is a crime punishable by imprisonment in Switzerland.

Dean Schlein was livid at my "stunt," placing me on probation along with orders to write a 20-page researched paper about the philosophy of lying.

Shortly thereafter, Chancellor was back at J. Press and asked to see me. He appeared sheepish and started to apologize when I gifted him a Shaggy Dog sweater and told him he'd provided my son with a lifetime experience together with a lesson in ethics. I also appreciated his compliments regarding my son's self-confidence.

J. Press and its celebrity clientele have enriched my life many times over, even though one of them nearly got my son thrown into a Swiss jail.

NUMBER 37

WE ARE COLLEGE GUYS

IN 1958, Larry Elliot, fellow Chi Phi at Dartmouth and trombonist leader of the Dartmouth Indian Chiefs Dixieland Band, wrote the music and co-authored the book and lyrics with yours truly for "The Chuck Sturdley Story," a one-act musical that brought down the house. Actually, several houses.

The show won a college prize for best presentation at the annual Interfraternity Play Contest and was subsequently offered a spot at a campus variety show, which was sponsored by the college in majestic Webster Hall, overlooking the Dartmouth Green, adjacent to Baker Library. The leading role of a romantically luckless plugger, Chuck Sturdley, was winsomely portrayed by fraternity brother John Hamilton Miller— post-college, John became a news editor for *The Wall Street Journal*.

Our frothy kerfuffle was a distant cousin of *Animal House*, scripted, coincidentally, by Dartmouth '62 alum Chris Miller.

Here is the blockbuster opening and closing number:

> *We are college guys, with bloody bloodshot eyes,*
> *Everybody loves us, so do we.*
> *Colorful 'til death, with whiskey on our breath,*

Dartmouth students pack Webster Hall.

THREADING THE NEEDLE II

Fraternity, virility, sexuality.
Inhibitions we hate
When seducing a date,
A clever remark,
A hand in the dark
Everything else can just wait.
Rah, Rah, Rah.

Singing and dancing and studiously romancing,
But to academic epidemics we're immune.
As students we admit
We're slightly out of fit,
But you can get an "A" in any way
If you remember to write in pen,
That's the reason
We are college men!

I recently spotted a newspaper squib reporting a contemplated Broadway musical production of *Animal House*. Should it ever come to pass and the producers care to co-opt our song, it's available.

NUMBER 38

IN LOVE WITH A SHAGGY DOG

WHEN I WAS a *pisher* growing up in New Haven, all the Yale big shots strutted up and down York Street showing off their light, natural Shaggy Dog sweaters, a source of unremitting envy. Grandpa Press gifted me my premier Shaggy Dog (size 36) when I entered first form at then Hopkins Grammar School. Together with my 37-regular J. Press Shetland sport coat, 14 by 32 OCBD, narrow wool challis necktie, plain-front grey flannel trousers, and Barrie Ltd. dirty white bucks, I was a primeval middle-school preppy.

As I entered the family business in 1959, J. Press prominently featured its famous Drumohr classic—original and incomparable soft, hand-brushed crew-neck pullovers, knitted on hand frames in Scotland with the finest Shetland wool in eight colors. "Light natural" was No. 1, capturing 40 percent of the Shaggy Dog sales.

Drumohr has long since expired. Nevertheless, current Shaggy Dogs more than meet their earlier match. Eight 1959 colors have been expanded to over a mind-boggling twenty.

Trust me, they're the real thing, and still redolent of the moors.

NUMBER 39

THE BEATLES, PINKERTON, AND J. PRESS

MADISON AND 44TH STREET wasn't strictly Camelot during the early 1960s. The thriving menswear retail neighborhood attracted swaths of shoplifters.

A daytime nightmare occurred on an otherwise uneventful early-spring morning when a perpetrator entered the store, brandishing a weapon and advising everybody to lie down and toss their wallets on the floor. As he bent down to pick up the loot, heroic (if not foolhardy) sales member Ralph Lauren–esque WASP archetype Ken Trommers grabbed his arm. The thief took off, but Ken followed in hot pursuit, eventually pinning the man against a wall across the street at Brooks Brothers. Turned out the weapon was a water pistol.

Fighting the scourge, J. Press hired a Pinkerton detective to secure the premises. Bill Ward filled the bill. Unobtrusive and vaguely professorial, he looked like a customer parading around the tie counter. Bill became so besotted with repps and tweeds that he left Pinkerton and became the J. Press official floorwalker, advising grateful Squeeze clients on their haberdashery choices.

This all occurred during the Beatles era. Turns out their manager lived above my apartment at Third Avenue and 73rd Street. The Liverpool sensation utilized the residence as a hide-

THREADING THE NEEDLE II

"Mr. Press," Bill asked, "how would your daughter like to meet the Beatles?"

away from riotous screaming Beatles lunatics.

Returning through the lobby one afternoon with my then four-year-old daughter, Jennifer, we were greeted by Bill Ward, assigned by Pinkerton to safeguard the group.

"Mr. Press," Bill asked, "how would your daughter like to meet the Beatles?"

Strawberry Fields forever.

NUMBER 40

THE OCBD OSCAR GOES TO J. PRESS

A RECENT BLOG POST in the revitalized *@ivy-style* under the direction of Bedford, New York, digital entrepreneur John Burton heralded the J. Press Oxford dress shirt—the Fundamental Staple.

The long journey to achieve this accolade started shortly before World War I, when my grandfather, the eponymous Jacobi Press, engaged in a button-down competition with non–New Haven competitor Brooks Brothers. John Brooks innovated his own version of the effervescent shirt favored by the British polo players he'd spotted as a fan on frequent buying trips to England at the turn of the twentieth century.

J. Press featured equivalent versions duly made in England under the auspices of furnishings-and-haberdashery supplier Welch Margetson. In the 1930s, as the winds of war diminished British sourcing, Grandpa turned to his pal Bernie Gantmacher, who had owned a shirt-and-pajama factory in New Haven since the 1920s. Bernie produced a reasonable facsimile, and as a favor Grandpa gave his sons Elliot and Marty jobs in the stockroom prior to their induction into the U.S. Army. While packing the ties and shirts and arranging the haberdashery in the York Street store, the Gantmacher boys inhaled the scent of Ivy, and the rest is history. They shortened their own name and the name of the business's, forming Gant Shirtmakers in 1949.

Meanwhile, the Press boys, Paul and Irving, uncomfortable sharing a national brand, searched out a private resource. Irving Press ran the Fort Ritchie PX store during World War II. Ralph Trishon, who ran a shirt factory with his brother in Norristown, Pennsylvania, supplied army-officer dress shirts for Irving's army-base post exchange. My uncle admired the quality and fit of the "Tyson Shirt" that became the prime J. Press shirt choice until their demise in the 1960s. They were followed by Troy Shirtmakers Guild of Glens Falls, New York. Troy Guild perpetuated the Made in USA 100 percent cotton button-down collar in our own barrel-cuff, full-bodied tradition.

I remember going head-to-head with Elliot and Marty at a party in New Haven sometime in the 1970s while visiting my parents. "We worked in your stockroom, and you only bought a few sport shirts from us," they said. "Good luck selling to our competitors," I replied. "We are happy for your success." The postprandial conversation continued merrily amongst the New Haven shirt cognoscenti, and I recall Gant competitor Seymour Shapiro, who broke away from the Gant brothers to form Sero Shirts, keeping his distance in the room.

Back to the *@ivy-style* Oscar. "The J. Press Oxford … read distinction. It looks like you spent the money … What it does here is create an Oxford shirt that carries itself with as much comfort as the pedigree it represents."

I could go on except for the fact of my drooling and eyes tearing. Access the blog and savor the rave.

NUMBER 41

BACK TO NEW YORK

MY LOVE AFFAIR with New York began soon after my four years at Dartmouth, which were followed by six months in the U.S. Army Reserves. After a stretch as an E-2 medic at Fort Sam Houston, Private Richard Press moved on to Fort Irving Press in the Big Apple. Filled with gusto for high times on the Ivy throne, I was demoted by Uncle Irving to a scrub, learning the business, adhering to unforgiving K.P. basic-training strictures supervised by General Irving E. Press. His clothing sophistication and knowledge provided a brilliant mix with his Yale Law School degree, leagues above and beyond his competitors in Ivy League quarters.

Our New York second-floor branch store was squeezed above the then quiescent northeast side of Madison Avenue and 44th Street. My gender-specific job description—salesman. Was it going to be my personal obit: *Death of a Salesman?*

> *"A salesman has got to dream, boy.*
> *It comes with the territory."*

A year after my initiation, that dream came true via our blockbuster move from our tenement situation to the high-ceilinged ground-floor emporium on the south side of 44th Street

J. PRESS

44th and Madison, "Grand Central Ivy."

between Fifth and Madison, soon tagged by the cognoscenti as "Grand Central Ivy."

J. Press enjoyed a hard-earned reputation by ensuring visits from a coterie of national celebrities—actors, entertainers, athletes, writers, business executives, politicians, and society figures. Irving Press assigned me to be anchorman at the door: "Hi, I'm Dick Press. How may we help you?"

After several subsequent moves, J. Press has found a permanent home with its groundbreaking 2018 relocation, fittingly side by side with the Yale Club on the corner of 44th and Vanderbilt.

NUMBER 42

LUCKY SEVEN IVY ESSENTIALS

THE SEVEN-YEAR ITCH brings me back to the "Ivy Style" exhibition, co-curated with my esteemed peer G. Bruce Boyer, at the Museum at the Fashion Institute of Technology in 2012, and attended by more than 50,000 visitors. An introduction for the unfamiliar, the show presented wardrobe essentials that delineated the heyday of Ivy, beginning in the early 1950s and awaiting glorious revival for our culturally dislocated times. We tend to forget a phrase that's no longer in the fashion vocabulary: "good taste." Ivy Style always represented excellent taste. It wasn't a symbol of economic superiority; it wasn't necessarily the dress of the wealthy—it's intergenerational. Which means it represents economic value. If you buy something that is traditionally Ivy Style, when you pull it out of the closet two years later, you don't think, 'Oh, that's what they wore ten years ago.' It could have been worn in 1955, 1985, or perhaps even nowadays. Here is my roster of seven Ivy League wardrobe essentials.

1. GREY SUIT: Many men today do not wear a suit every day, but there are certain occasions in a man's life that require a suit. And that doesn't mean they need a whole bunch of suits in their closet, but they do need one and possibly two, depending on

FORM 110

J PRESS INC
262 YORK STREET

WHEN REPLYING
REFER TO
NEW HAVEN
OFFICE

Gentlemen's Tailors and Furnishers
NEW HAVEN   CAMBRIDGE
NEW YORK

RE: Ivy League Wardrobe

---

1. Grey Suit
2. Blue Blazer
3. Grey Dress Slacks
4. Khakis
5. Oxford-Cloth Button-Down
6. Repp Tie
7. Loafers

their station in life and where they are going—maybe to a wedding, a funeral, an interview, or a business conference. To represent Ivy Style, it should be a grey suit—a blue suit is too formal for the daytime. I would suggest an old-fashioned grey solid suit or a grey chalk-stripe suit in mid-weight wool, perhaps a bit uncomfortable during the height of summer, but it works from September to June. It is the quintessential Ivy League Look.

2. BLUE BLAZER: A blue blazer with brass buttons can be worn with grey dress trousers for relatively formal occasions, or it can be dressed down with khakis, jeans, or corduroys. It also looks terrific with tartans or Nantucket reds.

3. GREY DRESS TROUSERS: A pair of grey mid-weight wool trousers are a classic Ivy Style look. They come in handy for more formal occasions when jeans or khakis just won't do.

4. KHAKIS: These are a must. Khakis are more signature to Ivy Style than jeans. I have nothing against jeans, but my personal preference is for khakis. They are the classic, informal pant—sturdy all-cotton twill with a flat front and quarter-top pockets. Credit veterans are flooding the Halls of Ivy, thanks to F.D.R.'s 1944 G.I. Bill of Rights for introducing them to Ivy League style.

5. OXFORD-CLOTH BUTTON-DOWN: If you look at pictures of President John Kennedy at the family compound in Hyannis Port, playing touch football, wearing Oxford button-down shirts with rolled-up sleeves and khaki trousers ... that's quintessential Ivy with Camelot frosting.

J. PRESS

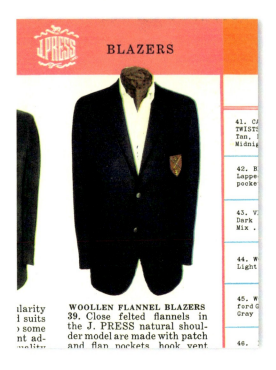

WOOLLEN FLANNEL BLAZERS
39. Close felted flannels in the J. PRESS natural shoulder model are made with patch and flap pockets, hook vent

6. REPP-STRIPE TIE: Are neckties going the way of fedora hats? What's going on with ties today? Except for TV anchors, many media figures are more often than not pictured without a tie. But from my view, I think it's gauche, to the worst degree, to wear a suit and a dress shirt without a tie. It looks sloppy and unfinished. To my way of thinking, particularly when ties today go for $75 and frequently more, a repp stripe represents the best value and can be worn with anything.

7. LOAFERS. Growing up in New Haven, along with thousands of Yalies, I got all my shoes at Barrie's, the shoe store located adjacent to J. Press. Our everyday favorite (to this day) is "penny" loafers in the dull brown, oxblood shade. Nope, never put a penny on the shoe. Sue me.

NUMBER 43

MR. SATURDAY NIGHT ON YORK STREET

JUST WENT MAD for the luminous performance by Billy Crystal starring in the terrific Broadway musical version of his 1992 film, *Mr. Saturday Night*, charting a comedian's up-and-down journey to fame and back that began as a Catskill Mountain hotel tummler, Yiddish for someone who stirs up tumult or excitement.

Billy Crystal's tragicomic performance brings to mind legendary York Street tummler George Feen, who touted his own New Haven Borscht Belt comic shtick on the Yale campus.

In an earlier column, I described George Feen's engaging jazz great Duke Ellington's enthusiasm for Dupioni silk tuxedos. Feen's underground enterprises serving time at J. Press took place more on York Street than in Harlem befriending Duke Ellington. Seeing *Mr. Saturday Night* rekindled my perhaps not-so-quaint memory of past times that, in its unique way, might also make a great musical with, maybe, Josh Gad playing George Feen.

"Little Georgie Feen," as he was known around town, operated in a Rashomon of hyperbolic deviltry. Insinuating himself with female pulchritude in the Yale Drama School, he once attached himself to a Lauren Bacall look-alike who was hip to his evil deeds. Feen fostered the libel that she was sexually

Billy Crystal's tragicomic performance brings to mind legendary York Street tummler George Feen.

THREADING THE NEEDLE II

liberated and longed to be hooked up with an Eli football player. She was in on the gag. Feen arranged a match for her with a Yale halfback. The thankful gridder returned the favor by giving Feen his tickets to the Harvard game. George then offered the 50-yard-line Yale Bowl Portal No. 16 tickets to the box-office manager of the Shubert Theatre in exchange for sold-out opening-night seats for the ensuing tryout of *South Pacific*.

Those, he funneled to a New Haven cop, who completed the ticket farrago by giving them to a Chapel Street liquor dealer he protected who sold booze under the table to Yale patrician fraternities, also meaning pledge masters steer his fraternity brothers back to Feen who took over draping them in J. Squeeze tweed. The penultimate heyday of Ivy roundelay.

A belt in the back meant more to Yalies than rear-trouser construction. It signaled partaking from a pint of Canadian Club in the back of J. Squeeze with "Little Georgie Feen."

Seventy years later, I still haven't recovered from the risqué Lauren Bacall look-alike pic he gifted me for my Bar Mitzvah.

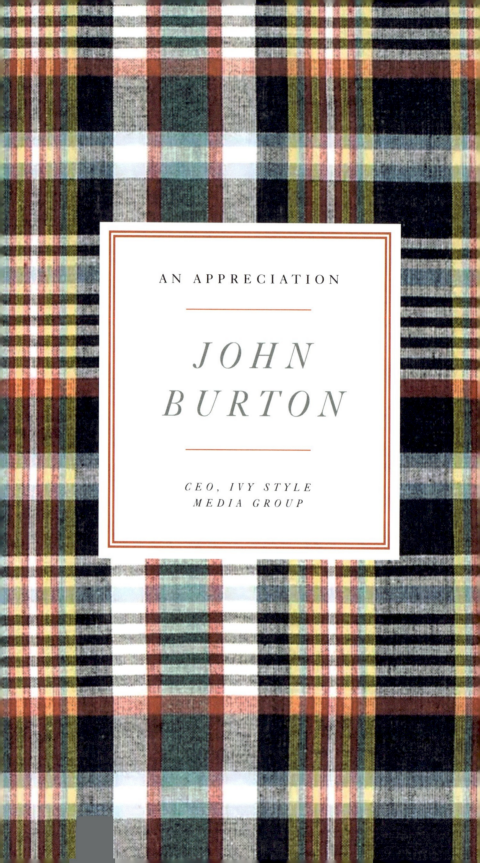

AN APPRECIATION

JOHN BURTON

CEO, IVY STYLE MEDIA GROUP

THE WORD "TOUCHSTONE" *comes from ... a stone. In the 15th century you held up your gold and silver against a piece of black quartz to determine its purity. When I first met Richard Press I had already been using his aesthetic as a touchstone for decades. Richard was due in minutes to present to media and customers and peers. Were it me, I'd have been behind a curtain flipping index cards like I was in poker game. Richard, the best-dressed man there (as voted by the readers of my site), instead spent the time making my 14-year-old daughter, the only child in attendance, comfortable. When he left to take the mic, she said, "Dad, I like him." I like him, too. And the company he carries the torch for. He's always effortlessly styled, affable, and humble. He's a family man, and the clothes of J. Press are his family crest. He's no joke, this is his DNA. Armed with his legacy, J. Press remarkably never veers off course. Richard Press is to be navigated by. Traditions need reference points. Commerce needs good people. We all need touchstones. We gratefully have all three in Richard Press and J. Press.*

NUMBER 44

BERMUDAS FOR THE
DOG DAYS OF SUMMER

HOW TO SURVIVE the dog days of August without looking like a slob? Jack Kennedy rolled up the sleeves of his cotton Oxford dress shirt and let it all hang out over his khaki walk shorts.

Bermuda shorts were the leisure summer garment of choice for the favored few in their salad days of the 1950s. After taking a Bermuda buggy ride with their best girl by their side, prep-school and college scions of the Establishment returned to campus for final exams from their rum-filled spring vacations, loaded to the gills with the real thing purchased at Trimingham's, the era's top-tier purveyor of the home product. J. Press got into the act in the early 1950s.

Best-selling author and cultural critic Lisa Birnbach put her stamp on the genre in her 1980 classic, *The Official Preppy Handbook*. The chapter titled "Dressing the Part" proclaimed, "Bermuda shorts are an integral part of a man's wardrobe. They are worn cut like dress trousers, only hemmed just above the knee. Solid cotton or madras."

More than 40 years later, J. Press continues to fill the bill with a world-class cornucopia of Bermuda shorts. Pick of the pack: seersucker, patchwork madras, pastels, and dark shades as well as varieties of cotton-madras plaids, poplins, stonewashed cotton chino, and batik prints.

WALK SHORTS

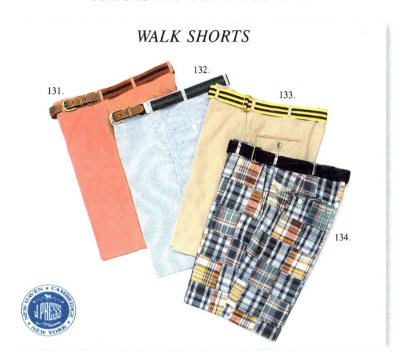

"Bermuda shorts are an integral part of a man's wardrobe."

The last word belongs to my friend, menswear historian and connoisseur G. Bruce Boyer, in his latest treatise, *True Style*, in which he dares to suggest, "Why not indeed wear a pastel chambray shirt, natty foulard bow tie, and lightweight blazer with a pair of Madras shorts?"

Bermudas go both ways.

NUMBER 45

BACK AT THE YALE CLUB

THE YALE CLUB, with which we share valued quarters, continues to stand tall directly across from Grand Central Terminal, in Midtown Manhattan.

Years ago, I was veep of the Dartmouth Club of New York, in the Yale Club, and in fact negotiated much of the sale of the family business to Onward Kashiyama in the now deposed Big Green lounge on the seventh floor. Other co-members of the Y.C. include fraternity D.K.E. (Delta Kappa Epsilon) and the University of Virginia. It's not all Boola Boola.

The Clubhouse was designed by James Gamble Rogers, '89, and hailed for its dignified neoclassical design. Upon opening its doors in 1915, the building became the largest clubhouse in the world and continues to be the largest college clubhouse in existence today.

Four other clubs affiliated with Ivy League universities have clubhouses in the surrounding neighborhood: the Harvard Club of New York, the Princeton Club of New York, the Penn Club of New York City, and the Cornell Club. The neighborhood also includes similar clubs not affiliated with universities, such as the New York Yacht Club and the University Club of New York.

The Yale Club's 22-story clubhouse contains three dining spaces (the Tap Room, the Grill Room, and the Roof Dining

The Yale Club.

Room and Terrace); four bars (in the Tap Room, Grill Room, Main Lounge, and on the Roof Terrace); banquet rooms for up to 500 people, such as the 20th-floor Grand Ballroom; 138 guest rooms; a library; the Fitness and Squash Center, which contains three international squash courts and a swimming pool; and a barbershop, among other amenities.

The heart of the Clubhouse is the Main Lounge, a large room with a high, ornate ceiling, large columns, and walls lined with fireplaces and portraits of the five Yale-educated U.S. presidents, all of whom are or were members of the Yale Club: William Howard Taft, Gerald R. Ford, George H. W. Bush, Bill Clinton, and George W. Bush.

Club wardrobe requirements remain extant: the House Committee requests that all members and guests observe the following dress requirements:

Traditional business attire or business casual dress, as defined below, is required in all public rooms except for the athletic facilities at all times. At all times a reasonable standard of neatness should be observed.

Business casual dress includes collared shirts, blouses, turtlenecks, sweaters, dress slacks, khakis, corduroy trousers, skirts, or dresses.

Denim: neat, clean, and in good repair (no holes, rips, or tears) – is permitted in the Library, Grill Room, Roof Dining Room, and on the weekends throughout the Clubhouse. All other above restrictions apply.

Not permitted: shorts, tee shirts, casual sandals, athletic wear of any kind (including sweatpants, caps, and team jerseys), and torn, provocative, or revealing clothing.

The beat goes on. Club members in the neighborhood historically serve as founts of tweed amongst our customer base.

NUMBER 46

J. PRESS & ALL THAT JAZZ

J. PRESS AND JAZZ, a syndrome I personally experienced during my misspent youth, although octogenarian memory of youthful high times begs forbearance with willing suspension of disbelief.

Before Elvis and the twist, jazz maestro Duke Ellington occupied the top of the charts after his triumphal appearance at the 1956 Newport Jazz Festival in ritzy Newport, Rhode Island. The Duke drove the concert crowd of thousands into a frenzy, prompting one of only five *Time* magazine covers dedicated to a jazz musician.

J. Press got into the act a couple of years before Newport. Our notorious and locally famous salesman George Feen, known around town as "Little Georgie Feen," respected no bounds. His tentacles even extended to Harlem when he finagled an introduction to Duke Ellington after a concert at the New Haven Arena. He showed the elegantly dressed bandleader silk-fabric books of Dupioni swatches. The Duke allowed him to take measurements after Little Georgie offered his J. Press business card, promising the gift of a silk dinner jacket made from the luxurious Dupioni silk swatch he'd selected.

Feen traveled to Harlem to deliver on his promise. Ellington loved the tuxedo and gave Feen more orders this time at the regular price. The patronage lasted several more years. A

Duke Elligton and Billy Strayhorn.

THREADING THE NEEDLE II

more enduring relationship occurred when Billy Strayhorn, the Duke's doppelgänger, arranger, and lyricist ("Take the A Train") admired the tuxedo and followed suit at the J. Press New York store for years thereafter, until his death in 1967.

The marriage between Dixieland jazz and Ivy, together with my own participation, was consummated by two sold-out concerts in Carnegie Hall during the 1955 Thanksgiving vacation my freshman year at Dartmouth. Princeton's Tiger Town Five, led by clarinetist Stan Rubin, who had appeared on *Tonight Starring Steve Allen* and previously gigged at Jimmy Ryan's. Their Friday-night concert also featured Eli's Chosen Six, from Yale.

The Saturday-night concert began with the Williams College Spring Street Stompers. The Indian Chiefs followed intermission before an infamously boisterous Dartmouth-loaded audience that summoned New York City police to stop the show and order a cease-and-desist to curb our enthusiasm.

The heyday of Ivy jazz is best recalled in *The Great Gatsby*, by F. Scott Fitzgerald, Princeton idol of the flapper era:

> *All night the saxophones wailed the*
> *hopeless comment of the Beale Street Blues*
> *while a hundred pairs of golden and*
> *silver slippers shuffled the shining dust.*

NUMBER 47

SALTY VIBES

THE PREPPY 1980S are gone with the wind. *The Official Preppy Handbook* author, speaker, and humorist Lisa Birnbach memorably offered the era's final beachwear lesson in her preppy bible: "Madras swim trunks. Plain and boxy. The prep man has no interest in looking daring or sexy on the beach. Because they are made of cotton, they never fully dry out if they are used daily."

Times may have changed but not the look. J. Press currently offers a cornucopia of swim trunks uniquely suited for beach-club or urban-weekend wear. Available in varieties of all-cotton India madras, seersucker, and patchwork fabrics, with mesh liner, elasticized waist for comfort, rear button through flap pocket and side pockets.

Our revised Heyday Look swim trunks open a new door to a wider audience that once was the restricted province of St. Grottlesex snobs, Ivy League elites, and Hyannis Port Kennedys.

Alfred Hitchcock shot a famous scene for his 1955 masterpiece, *To Catch a Thief*, with J. Press Shaggy Dog sweater aficionado Cary Grant on the French Riviera in boxer-style trads side by side lithe Grace Kelly, tightly wrapped in a one-piece swimsuit.

J. PRESS Swim Wear goes both ways—for an ocean splash on Georgica Beach emitting the salty vibes of a dirty martini or drying out for a post-swim jaunt to grab a lobster roll and a couple of brews at Duryea's Lobster Deck in Montauk.

Snazzy and dry-docked in J. Squeeze India madras swim trunks. Salty vibes.

122. Butcher Blue/White heavy block stripes, with zip fly, adjustable ringed side tabs, distinctive interlock front buckle, button flap pocket and self-supporter $12.50

VYCRON/COTTON
COOLIE CLOTHS

123. Zipper fly-front model with adjustable ringed side tabs, button flap pocket and self-supporter. Solid Duffel Blue, Breton Brick, and Duffel Green $13.50

STRIPED COTTON
COOLIE CLOTH

124. Tailored as #123 above, but with extra long legs. Duffel Blue & White Blazer stripes with solid Duffel Blue waistband $12.50

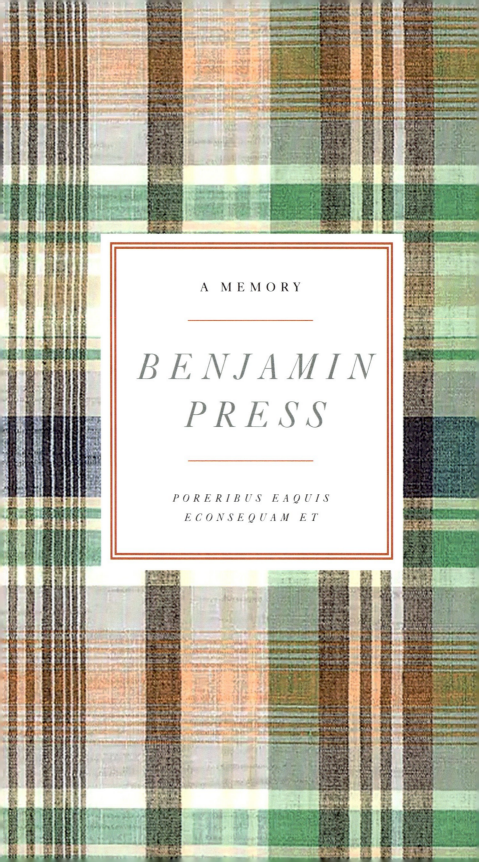

LIKE A MASTER VINTNER, *my father waited for my maturation, that ephemeral moment in graduating me from boys' sizes at Brooks Brothers. I remember at age fourteen anticipating when Dad would deem me ready to be tapped into sartorial manhood. The mandate of my alma mater, The Buckley School, called for blue blazers, grey flannels, corduroys (thin-lined or "wide whale"), and khakis.*

In 1980, Dad summoned me to "the store", as we in the family colloquially referred to it. He ushered me in the back to Felix, the famed (within J. Press circles) tailor whose reputation for having fitted Sinatra, Bush, Redford, etc. was legendary. Felix was a giant despite barely reaching my height. An Auschwitz survivor, his tailoring skills saved his life being deemed "useful" for his skill in stitching Gestapo uniforms. That day he wielded his needle like a Stradivarius. Felix chalked lines up the back of my blazer, down the seam of my slacks, across the shoulder of the jacket ... I was his canvas and he conjured a masterpiece of perfect fit.

My first fitting remains an indelible memory. Dad ushered me through a right of passage he had experienced thirty years prior. It was a proud moment that "Press men," both familial and beyond, have been going through for more than a century.

NUMBER 48

SUITING UP ELI FROSH

SUITING UP Eli frosh in the heyday of Ivy was do-or-die for New Haven clothiers. Salesmen at J. Press were instructed by my dad, Paul Press (front right), to memorize the *Yale Freshman Blue Book*. He quizzed them daily about dorm addresses, hometowns, and secondary schools the book provided. Yale freshmen lived in seven ancient dormitories on the Old Campus. The favored boarding choice was Durfee Hall, with its communal suites designed to house six to nine students and mainly populated by St. Grottlesex elites.

My father's older brother, Irving Press (seated, left)—Yale Law School, class of 1926—ran the family business out of New York. He was a mainstay at the Yale Club next door to the company offices, then on 44th Street, and the blood that surged through his arteries was Yale Blue. The Press brothers utilized their private Yale C.I.A. info to get the J. Press crew on the inside track.

Little Georgie Feen (standing, left), popularly known to the cognoscenti as the "Mayor of York Street," knocked on every door in Durfee Hall, offering his calling card, sample swatches, booze, and a promise of favors. Georgie was a small "d" democrat, serving anybody who walked into the store, whether they were "white shoe" or Podunk High.

Salesmen at J. Press were instructed by my dad, Paul Press, to memorize the Yale Freshman Blue Book.

Goodbye to New Orleans, a memoir by Peter Wolf, recalls coming to Yale from Exeter. Wolf's roommate turned out to be Calvin "Bud" Trillin, then a virgin outlander from Kansas City, later in life a celebrated American journalist, food writer, poet, fellow memoirist, and novelist. Trillin lamented to Wolf, "We couldn't find the Ivy-look, eastern-type clothes in Kansas City that people wear here, so my folks decided I'd buy some new stuff when I got to Yale. Where do you suggest I go? Five minutes later we were inside J. Press, a couple of blocks away on York Street.

Under the hovering, appraising eye of George Feen, one of the great haberdashery salesmen of all time, Bud replaced key parts of his wardrobe."

Herman Racow (standing, right) was the acknowledged elder statesman of 262 York Street. He was constantly combing his full stack of index cards to identify any incoming offspring of his alumni "see you's."

Gabe Giaquinto (standing, second from right), with roots in the Italian-American Wooster Street neighborhood, bounded by Sally's and Frank Pepe's pizza parlors and cashed in, deploying his ownership of local non-WASPs.

Sam Kroop (standing, second from left) achieved tournament celebrity at the Yale Golf Course ever since caddying as a teenager at Hillhouse High. He picked up country-club gossip about incoming Bulldog duffers. Sam was also the West Coast J. Press road traveler, collecting names of all his customers' offspring who were heading back east to college.

New Haven was Boomtown Ivy from the end of World War II until the conflagrations erupting in the late 1960s. During the heyday, hundreds of tailors, salespersons, shippers, and shleppers ruled the roost. Thousands of Yalies roamed Elm City byways garbed in J. Press three-button suits, Shetland sport coats, plain-front grey flannel trousers, OCBDs, three-inch-width neckties, Shaggy Dog sweaters anchored by dirty white bucks—the ephemera of New Haven's golden age.

Looking back through memory's eyes
We will know life has nothing sweeter than its springtime,
Golden Days when we were young.

NUMBER 49

INSIDER TRADING AND IRISH OYS

THE PARDON awarded to convicted financier Mike Milken in February of 2020 recalls my appearance on the Off Off Broadway stage with another jailbird, arbitrageur and J. Press customer Ivan Boesky. Milken's fate was originally determined when Boesky pleaded guilty to securities fraud, implicating Milken's insider-trading stock manipulation.

"Oy, dot muzt be de texxis cab" was my stage character's opening line, in response to a honking car offstage as the curtain rose on the 1976 Van Dam Theatre revival of the 1920s vintage classic *Abie's Irish Rose.*

One of the demands of my leading role as well-to-do immigrant widower Solomon Levy was affecting a Yiddisher dialect, a chore I was eminently familiar with from memories of dear Grandma Jenny Press (wife of J. Press founder Jacobi) and her struggles with the English language, often sending my cousin David and me into hysterics that would prompt a slap on the puss from angry mother, Aunt Marion.

The Off Off Broadway showcase production was sold out for all its eight performances, thanks to cast member Boesky, corporate-takeover speculator. A decade later, the December 1, 1986, cover of *Time* magazine featured his prominence in the Wall Street insider-trading scandals of the 1980s. Thanks to a plea

The review regaled "Irish Oys," calling Ivan's performance "amusing."

bargain, he served only two years of his three-and-a-half-year sentence at California's Federal Correctional Institution Lompoc, along with coughing up a $100 million fine.

I met Ivan in the early seventies, when he was a fellow member of my beloved, and now long gone, City Athletic Club. During its ninety-year run, City A.C. was the respected West 54th Street Jewish equivalent of the New York Athletic Club. Ivan regularly preyed upon its four squash courts, spending hours strategizing his game with the club pro. Beside his squash talents, he possessed an eccentric wit, nourished in childhood behind the counter at his father's Detroit delicatessen. The Boesky pastrami-on-rye genes prompted our Borscht Belt repartee, where we played off each other at the club's second-floor bar.

Ivan also showed off an extensive J. Press wardrobe of similar midnight grey, clear-finish worsted suits, always paired with semi-formal starched, white, broadcloth straight-collar shirts against English Macclesfield, Spitalsfield, or Swiss-lace, grenadine silk ties.

One afternoon after a shvitz and swim in the club's fifth-floor lap pool, he tossed me a question. "Richard, doing any theater lately?" I filled him in on my role in the upcoming production of *Abie's Irish Rose*. Ivan's face lit up. "I love acting. Anything in it for me?" I gave him the phone number of the director, who called me shortly thereafter. "Hey, this guy Boesky is a scream. I gave him the part of your nosy neighbor, Isaac Cohen."

Run-throughs took place after closing hours at J. Press, 16 East 44th Street. We rehearsed stage business in the mezzanine amidst sport coats and trousers, adjacent to the shipping room with senior J. Press shipping clerk Clifford White, busily packing suits for the next day's UPS delivery.

Limousines blocked the Vandam Street Theatre entrance, disgorging Ivan F. Boesky & Company customers, who poured into the shabby Lower East Side 120-seat venue that defined 1970s Off Off Broadway.

My interlude from J. Press was well received by trade-paper *Show Business*. The review regaled "Irish Oys," calling Ivan's performance "amusing." The critic continued, "Richard Press has a magnetic and endearing quality as Solomon Levy."

After the curtain came down and the stage lights dimmed, I returned to peddling tweeds. As for Ivan Boesky:

Oy, don't ask.

NUMBER 50

IT ALL STARTS WITH A GOOD FOUNDATION

PERHAPS AT SOME FUTURE TIME, historians will refer to *Threading the Needle* for cultural insight regarding the heyday of Ivy in the same way the preppy saga is characterized by its witty litterateur Lisa Birnbach, who declared boxer shorts as the male underwear of choice:

> *"Big, baggy and long. It is not entirely ludicrous, in Prep circles, for the bottom of a man's boxers to peep out from time to time beneath his Bermuda shorts. The boxers are made of cotton. White or solid pastels. The man may be given tartan plaid shorts as a gift, but only by a woman."*

My daughter, Jennifer Press Marden, gets into the act for an inside bit included in my previous 200-plus-page opus, in which I recall her visits to her dad's 44th Street emporium:

"A few boxer shorts in my J. Press bags later (I am not going to proclaim I invented boxers as pajamas at boarding schools across the Northeast) us girls got a dose of how the sausage (kosher) was made."

The beat goes on. As commander in chief of Ivy Style, J. Press headlines the boxer tradition: "It all starts with a good foundation." Reaching into its 119-year merchandise archives,

THREADING THE NEEDLE II

the company identified by my grandpa's signature today curates a selection of boxers that includes broadcloth, oxford, and end-on-end in solids and stripes. All still proudly made in the U.S.A. Imagine carrying the flag of an era under your pants.
Oh, the humanity!

SPECIAL THANKS

Laura Arnold, John Burton, Jack Carlson,
Ted Harrington, Scott Hill, Jason Jules, Patricia Mears,
Jun Murakami, Yuki Okita, Mark Oppenheimer,
Benjamin Press, Andrew Schoomaker, John Segal,
Robert Squillaro, and Michael Williams

CREDITS

PAGE XI © *Lotta Studio*
PAGE XIV *Andrew Schoomaker*
PAGE 20 *Bettmann/via Getty Images*
PAGE 23 *Hulton Archive/via Getty Images*
PAGE 25 *Archive Photos/via Getty Images*
PAGE 28 *Courtesy of New Haven Register*
PAGE 32 *Courtesy of Newman Architects*
PAGE 34 *Hulton Archive/via Getty Images*
PAGE 41 *Courtesy of Press Family*
PAGE 44 *Moviepix /via Getty Images*
PAGE 49 *Kohei Kawashima*
PAGE 52 *Hulton Archive/via Getty Images*
PAGE 56 *Courtesy of Press Family*
PAGE 57 *Kohei Kawashima*
PAGE 64 *Courtesy of Dartmouth College Library*
PAGE 73 *Courtesy of Press Family*
PAGE 75 *Laura Arnold*
PAGE 78 *Courtesy of Dartmouth College Library*
PAGE 81 *GL Archive/via Almy Stock Photos*
PAGE 90 *Masataka Suemitsu*
PAGE 92 *Bettmann/via Getty Images*
PAGE 94 *Archive Photos/via Getty Images*
PAGE 96 *Archive Photos/via Getty Image*
PAGE 99 *Courtesy of Harvardband.org*
PAGE 101 *Courtesy of Press Family*
PAGE 104 *Hulton Archive/via Getty Images*
PAGE 106 *Bettmann/via Getty Images*
PAGE 118 *Disney General Entertainment Content/via Getty Images*
PAGE 124 *Masataka Suemitsu*
PAGE 127 *Hulton Archive/via Getty Images*
PAGE 134 *Bettmann/via Getty Images*
PAGE 138 *Courtesy of Dartmouth College Library*
PAGE 143 *New York Daily News/via Getty Images*
PAGE 145 *Masataka Suemitsu*
PAGE 164 *Michael Ochs Archive/via Getty Images*
PAGE 174 *Courtesy of Press Family*
PAGE 177 *Masataka Suemitsu*
PAGE 182 *Andrew Schoomaker*

ABOUT THE AUTHOR

Richard Press, the grandson of J. Press founder Jacobi Press, worked at the family company from 1959 to 1991, eventually serving as president. He also spent four years as president and C.E.O. of F. R. Tripler & Co. A graduate of the Loomis Chaffee School, Dartmouth College, and the American Academy of Dramatic Arts, he holds a master's degree from the New York Institute of Technology. Richard lives with his wife, Vida, in Manhattan.